DEEP
SHALLOW
DIVE into
YOU

How to have a more Authentic
Relationship with Yourself

Written by

Ray Doustdar
Host

Available on all Platforms + YouTube + our Website
WWW.DEEPSHALLOWDIVE.COM
@DEEPSHALLOWDIVE

For permission requests, write to the publisher using the email address below.

legal@deepshallowdive.com | www.deepshallowdive.com

First Edition

ISBN eBook: 978-0-9601255-0-0
ISBN Paperback: 978-0-9601255-1-7
ISBN Hardcover: 978-0-9601255-2-4

Library of Congress Control Number: 2024907414

CALLING A SPADE A SPADE

DEEP
SHALLOW
DIVE into
YOU

How to have a more Authentic
Relationship with Yourself

Written by

Ray Doustdar

In Dedication:

To my Dad.

Even though we did not know it then, one of the last things you said to me was, *"I am always with you,"* …and you have been and continue to be.

As the years pass, my appreciation and gratitude deepen for your selflessness and sacrifices for my brother and me. Every day, I strive to embody the values you've instilled in us. This book is a testament to your profound insight and critical thinking—a humble tribute and lasting memorial to honor your enduring mark on our lives.

Thank you for being our Dad.

You are dearly loved and missed.

I also dedicate this book to the cherished memory of three dear friends who left us far too soon: Kevin Kelly, Dave Hebenstreit, and Jackson Rohm. You are deeply loved and profoundly missed by many.

Til we meet again.

its okay

to begin your story today.

Those mistakes you've made along the way
are lessons, not failures. You were meant to
get back up and find a way, another path.

There is no expiration date to
reinventing yourself.

Ray Doustdar

@deepshallowdive

Table of Contents:

BE AUTHENTIC WITH YOURSELF.

Chapter 1:

LIFE.
Uncomfortable Truths.

Stay inspired.
Never stop trying.

@DEEPSHALLOWDIVE

Chapter 1: LIFE.
Uncomfortable Truths.

Sometimes, the hardest thing in life is admitting to an uncomfortable truth. It's a simple statement, yet it carries the weight of an entire universe of unspoken feelings, unresolved issues, and the very essence of what it means to be human. This *Uncomfortable Truth* for me started in March 2020.

To be exact, it started on Friday, March 13, 2020. That was the day the President of the United States declared a National Emergency concerning the Novel Coronavirus Disease Outbreak. The world changed. Life as we knew it changed. And I started to change.

Don't worry; this book is not about any of that. Not at all. But it is about the awakening that this March 2020 event caused in me and the awakening that I hope this book can trigger in you. Here is my goal with this book: *I want you to have a more authentic relationship with yourself.* That's it.

To paraphrase the great Steve Jobs, "I want you to realize that everything that takes place in this life is made by people who are no smarter than you are." Think about what he said. It's true. They're not any more intelligent than you. Their senses might just be more awake.

So, I want to help you awaken all your senses.

I want to help you awaken YOU.

Ok, enough about you, now let's get back to me! Hopefully, you will also laugh while reading this book.

As the days unfolded in March 2020, what started as a weekend at home continued indefinitely. Then it happened. For some reason, the rise of these three simple words, which immediately captured the world's attention, uniquely resonated with me. For me, the idea of *Flatten the Curve* didn't just help slow down the virus; that phrase and its implications started to expand my mind.

To refresh your memory, *Flatten the Curve* was a phrase used at the beginning of the COVID-19 pandemic. It referred to the goal of slowing the spread of the virus to prevent healthcare systems from being overwhelmed.

I remember that first weekend when we were all advised to limit our outdoor activities and stay indoors as much as possible. That felt different to me. It felt uncomfortable and strange as I had never experienced anything like that here in the United States of America, the land of limitless freedom.

But the genuinely thought-provoking part was that although being told to stay inside my home felt strange, it also served as a wake-up call.

It made me start reading the news obsessively, googling everything I could think of while the local or cable news kept playing in the background, and paying much more attention to the world than ever.

Rather than just letting it happen, I was obsessed with figuring out what was happening. This obsession caused me to think more, learn, and see the world differently. My newfound thirst to try and figure out what was going on has continued to this day.

In hindsight, I'm thankful. Very thankful. This new inquisitive mindset became an opportunity for personal growth and a chance to transform my understanding of the world.

Before that Friday night, I cruised through life on autopilot regarding politics and world affairs. "I hate Politics," said everyone, including me.

But the magnitude of this event was different, and it was something we had never experienced in our lifetimes. Life as we knew it would change within weeks, and I felt myself changing. But now, I was changing with both eyes wide open and looking at things differently.

This book stems from my *Deep Shallow Dive* into these politics and world affairs and what has occurred since March 2020.

But my *Deep Shallow Dive* has become so much more than that. It has become about ME, and now it is about YOU.

So, what exactly is a ***Deep Shallow Dive?***

Consider it a straightforward approach that simplifies a complex and significant concept into an easily understandable explanation.

The ***Deep*** part is about getting to know the heart of the matter.

The ***Shallow*** part means you stay mindful of information overload.

The ***Dive*** part is about delving into the topic to grasp the essentials and truly understand it.

Although it has nothing to do with water or scuba diving, it's like snorkeling — you go underwater to see amazing things and enjoy, but you stay close to the surface so you can always come back up for air. This method lets you truly understand something essential but in a clear and non-overwhelming way.

What emerged hand in hand with this newfound *Deep Shallow Dive* A.K.A. DSD mentality also became the concept of *calling a Spade a Spade*. This phrase is not new. *Calling a Spade a Spade* originated in ancient Greece and became prominent in the 16th century.

Over time, *calling a Spade a Spade* became a popular English idiom used to describe speaking frankly and directly without mincing words or sugarcoating the truth. It's about being straightforward and honest, even if the truth might hurt or be uncomfortable.

For some reason, with everything that was going on, that phrase resonated with me. It still does. And this book is that.

This book is a *Deep Shallow Dive*.

This book will *Call a Spade a Spade*.

These pages will explore personal relationships, business relationships, geopolitics, and social issues that are now everywhere. We will also explore our health and wellness, family life, and relationships with others and ourselves to understand better how to change the status quo and live our truth, even when it's uncomfortable.

This book is about YOU. It's about ME.

We will *dive* into this obsession with cell phones; seriously, we are obsessed with them.

Dive into why we feel the need to reply right away. *Dive* into why we expect immediate gratification.

Dive into why we look at our phone while in the bathroom (wow, I do that. Insert hand-to-face emoji), why we look at our phone while in bed, while at a traffic light, while at dinner in a restaurant, when someone gets up from the table, between sets at the gym, while walking on the street, sometimes while crossing the street, and even while watching TV. I am guilty of all that.

Wow. Seriously, I do all those. Do you?

Please say yes.

March 2020 was the birth of my starting to DSD into myself, and I hope the same for you after reading this book.

It was also the birth of me embracing *calling a Spade a Spade* in various aspects of my life and with myself. I hope the same for you after reading this book.

What started as me being focused on geopolitics caused me to become focused on ME.

My life. My family.

My friends. My relationships.

My health. My body.

My career. My thoughts.

My views. My desires.

My aspirations. My passions.

My insecurities. My feelings.

And even my regrets.

That's been the toughest one, and I won't even lie. My regrets because I have them. But I recognize that now, and identifying those regrets helps me deal with them.

This book, *Deep Shallow Dive into YOU*, is an internal call to action, a journey into your heart and inner core, and an exploration of the transformative power of embracing your uncomfortable truths.

It's a reminder that sometimes, the hardest thing in life is the essential thing—confronting reality instead of moving on to the next issue without resolution.

It reminds us to look at things as they are, not as we want them to be.

It's about diving into the uneasiness and understanding the power of facing our truths instead of being sidetracked by the next distraction.

We'll explore how confronting the uncomfortable can change our personal and professional relationships, social and political views, health, family life, and much more.

There is a page at the end of every Chapter for you to jot down notes or thoughts.

Lastly, I have just one ask:

As you read this book, please put down your phone and join me on this ride of depth and self-discovery. Let's break free from interruptions and the habit of avoiding being present.

Let's embrace a future where candid truth, brutal honesty when needed, and unfiltered transparency lead to a more profound, authentic, and meaningful life.

> **EVERYBODY HAS IDEAS.**
>
> **NOT EVERYBODY MAKES THEM HAPPEN.**

Ray Doustdar

@deepshallowdive

Chapter End Notes

Chapter 2:

ME.
A Personal Reflection.

Stay engaged.
Never stop helping
others.

BE AUTHENTIC WITH YOURSELF.

@DEEPSHALLOWDIVE

Chapter 2: ME.
A Personal Reflection.

As I mentioned, in March 2020, the world was thrust into unprecedented uncertainty. *Flatten the Curve* echoed across media channels and government declarations, serving as a rallying cry to curb the spread of a novel and highly contagious virus. The world needed collective action and unity to address a rapidly evolving crisis.

However, this simple call to action sparked something more profound in me—an unsettling feeling that there was more beneath the surface. While the idea of flattening the curve was presented as a straightforward solution to a pressing problem, it didn't sit right with my innate sense of inquiry, skepticism, and, more than anything, my common sense.

It wasn't the phrase per se; it was the recommended and often required course of action. I'm not saying they were wrong, although hindsight does allow us that luxury. It just felt different and made me pay attention, like when your teacher called your name, and you were daydreaming. You suddenly start paying attention.

This discomfort, born from questioning the simplicity of the narrative, marked the beginning of my process to *Expand My Mind*. It was a realization that the world's complexities couldn't be distilled into a single catchphrase. There was a yearning to understand the *deeper* layers of the situation, to go beyond page one in Google and the opening segment of the evening news, and grapple with the potential and uncomfortable truths lurking behind these. Or in all honesty, if nothing else, at least dig in a little and see if there were any.

As I delved into the complexities of the pandemic, its impact on society, and the response of governments and media, I discovered that the world was far from black and white. I have always known this, but I never thought about it. I mean, I never thought about it and tried to understand it.

But now, societal uncomfortable truths started emerging—such as the vulnerabilities in our healthcare systems, the disparities in access to resources in various communities, the ethical dilemmas faced by our decision-makers, and the myriad of social and economic repercussions that all these could cause.

Quickly, I realized that this awakening I was experiencing wasn't just about the pandemic; it extended to a broader perspective on life itself. I could expand my understanding of everything by understanding the world's complexities and embracing its uncomfortable truths. The current situation expanded my knowledge of other topics and, eventually, of myself. Expanding my mind was about venturing *deeper* than the surface, seeking out diverse viewpoints, and acknowledging that the world could be more complex and complicated than I could ever fathom.

My experience, which started in March 2020, taught me the importance of not accepting things at face value, rather questioning them and having the courage to confront the potentially uncomfortable truths—even when they challenge the narratives presented by authorities or the mainstream that I had been trained to trust naturally. I'm telling you, this is not bad. It's not. It all comes from a good place. A place of common sense and seeking clarity and understanding. It also should not be controversial. Remember what Steve Jobs said? Well, that applies here as well.

Fueled by initial discomfort and curiosity, this awakening became my catalyst for personal growth and a fundamental driver of my desire to *Deep Shallow Dive* into everything. It reflected that embracing uncomfortable truths is not bad and is a path to *deeper* understanding, personal transformation, and a more authentic engagement with the world.

In essence, my experiences starting in March 2020 were the spark that ignited my commitment to exploring my uncomfortable truths, expanding my mind, and now encouraging others to do the same through these pages. They were a compelling reminder that uncomfortable yet meaningful conversations are sometimes necessary to question, learn, and confront the multifaceted nature of our world and lives.

So, how did this all start? How did *Deep Shallow Dive* start?

My road to DSD and exploring the concept of *calling a Spade a Spade* had a humble beginning. It was rooted in my desire to make sense of the world and spark meaningful conversations. It all started with posts on various platforms, mainly Instagram and Facebook.

In hindsight, it's funny to look back now at those because it was also the first time I was dipping into the waters of controversy on social media. Before this, I posted mainly health-related things centered around my liquid vitamin business and fresh vegetable juicing, cute pictures of my niece and nephew, or pictures where my hair looked good. I'm joking. I'm not joking!

At the outset, I used humor as a powerful tool to convey a more profound message. Through clever memes, witty images, and humorous content, I sought to draw attention to the often perplexing and nonsensical aspects I saw going on.

However, these posts were not just about entertainment; they were a form of social commentary, highlighting the contradictions and discomforting truths beneath the surface of everyday life throughout 2020 and even 2021.

Here is an example. I posted this on April 16, 2020, which makes me laugh now. FYI, my signature 'look' in fashion was wearing a vest. I wore vests, and my network knew that!

So here is that post:

Actual Post

4/16 2020

raydoustdar
Los Angeles, California

Day 33... of me NOT wearing a Vest. This is Madness.

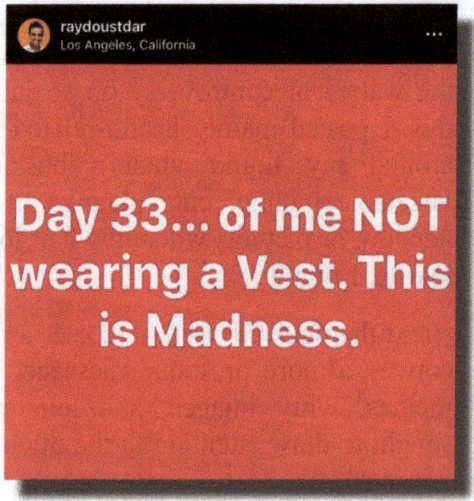

And it was madness! Thirty-three days without wearing a Vest. That was unprecedented.

In addition to just giving my friends a laugh, the essence of these early posts was to poke funny yet innocent jabs at things and prompt people to think about what was happening. They were amusing and subtle but had intention. At that time, though, I was not trying to do anything besides urge others to stop and again think about things. I wanted people to recognize the inconsistencies and complexities going unnoticed in the rush of the daily barrage of new information.

As these posts started gaining traction and resonating with an ever-growing audience, I felt compelled to broaden my approach to connect with more people. I continued the humorous posts and then supplemented those with longer and more detailed stories on Instagram and Facebook. These stories served as a platform for *deeper* exploration, allowing me to delve into further complex subjects, dissect things a little more, and try to engage readers in thought-provoking scenarios.

They also served as my first foray into storytelling. Each story would have multiple slides, usually three to five, thus allowing me more space and an opportunity to tell a more complete story. IG/FB Stories also allowed me to end with a message or takeaway I wanted them to have.

For two years, from March 2020 until the end of 2022, these social media posts and stories became a platform for me to refine my perspective and connect with a community of individuals who shared a similar curiosity and thirst for understanding.

Instagram has an archive feature that allows you to view all your stories, which is very cool. As research for this book, I went back and looked at all the Posts and Stories I had created, and wow, there were so many. Here is an ironic Story post as we entered 2023 that is interesting to see now with hindsight.

I posted this on January 1, 2023.

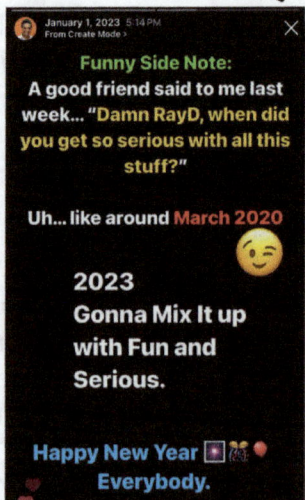

As we entered the new year, the concept of DSD became even more collaborative, as readers and followers actively participated in discussions and debates sparked by the content. Friends started messaging me, saying, "You should start a Podcast!" I would always reply, "Thanks, I appreciate that. Maybe I will!"

Well, I did.

The natural progression from Posts to Posts + Stories finally led to the creation of the *Deep Shallow Dive Podcast*, which launched in August 2023. This addition has allowed me to amplify my discussions, engage in more in-depth conversations about uncomfortable truths, and pull clips from other people and media to reinforce the episodes' content.

The DSD Podcast has become a platform for candid conversations, where I explore current and past topics, challenge prevailing narratives, and encourage listeners to think critically. It continues today. If you are so inclined, take 30 seconds to look at your phone and subscribe to the *Deep Shallow Dive Podcast*, available everywhere you listen to podcasts. Shameless plug, I know. But it's good, I promise.

Okay. Here's a quick progression recap: The global situation led to the posts, which led to the stories, which led to the podcast, which led to this book. That's seriously how it happened. It makes me laugh laying it out like that, but that was the progression.

In essence, what inspired me to embark on the *Deep Shallow Dive* concept was a profound sense that the world was rife with inconsistencies and uncomfortable truths that deserved attention.

I have shed light on these issues through humor, storytelling, and candid conversations, encouraging others to explore a more authentic and discerning perspective on our world.

The story began with social media posts but has evolved into a transformative platform and, hopefully, a community for embracing uncomfortable truths and *Calling a Spade a Spade*.

In short, the events of March 2020 shook the world, bringing with them a stark realization that we were living in unprecedented uncertainty.

Amidst this chaos and uncertainty, I discovered a silver lining. It was an awakening, a realization that, in many ways, I had been navigating life in an unaware state, unaware of the intricate threads connecting global events to my existence.

That call to *Flatten the Curve* became an unintentional call to expand my mind.

This period of uncertainty gave birth to *Deep Shallow Dive*, a metaphorical plunge into the depths of understanding geopolitics and, in turn, understanding myself.

It was a profound recognition that being informed about global affairs made me pay attention to the complexities of the world and then pay attention and start thinking about the complexities within my own life.

Through this experience, I gained a newfound appreciation for our world's duplicity and recognized the transformative power of embracing uncomfortable truths.

This became more than a wake-up call; it became my new approach to life. It was a realization that by understanding the painful realities of the world, I could better navigate the intricacies of my realities.

From there, I could engage more meaningfully in political conversation, contribute to resolving pressing social issues, or use social media to share my viewpoints, which are now my own. Those are the byproducts of having informed and researched viewpoints.

This was my journey to DSD and learning to *call a Spade a Spade* — of facing uncomfortable truths head-on and allowing them to shape a more conscious and authentic existence for myself.

As you embark on this exploration through the pages of *Deep Shallow Dive into YOU*, I hope you will find the desire to confront your uncomfortable truths, deepen your understanding of yourself, and foster positive change in your life.

This book is also an invitation to break free from the tendency of avoidance, to challenge things, and to embark on a voyage of self-discovery and personal transformation. It acknowledges that sometimes the most challenging thing in life is also the most transformative—admitting that uncomfortable truth.

Before we move forward, I want to plant some seeds.

These seeds are the pillars of the foundation of integrity I have built with myself. Embracing them has led to personal growth, helped me have better conversations, and given me a structure to analyze things.

Here are the four pillars of *Deep Shallow Dive*:

Self-awareness: *Self-awareness* is the ability to acknowledge one's weaknesses, biases, and areas needing improvement, which requires introspection and self-reflection. We can identify areas for change and development by confronting uncomfortable truths about ourselves. Heightened *self-awareness* is the first step toward personal growth.

Resilience: Facing uncomfortable truths can be emotionally challenging but also builds *resilience*. We develop emotional *resilience* when acknowledging our vulnerabilities and navigating through difficult emotions. This strength enables us to cope with adversity and bounce back from setbacks.

***Authenticity*:** This is a big one for me. Embracing uncomfortable truths often means letting go of pretenses and living authentically. This *authenticity* allows us to connect with others more deeply, as we are seen as genuine and trustworthy. It leads to more meaningful relationships.

And most important of all, ***Empathy:*** Confronting uncomfortable truths often involves recognizing the experiences and perspectives of others. This process fosters compassion. *Empathy* makes you see both sides. It's an excellent quality to have.

Here are some definitions that bring these to life:

/DSD Self-Awareness

"conscious knowledge of one's own character, feelings, motives, and desires."

DSD PILLARS
self·a·ware·ness

/DSD Resilience

"the process and outcome of successfully adapting to difficult or challenging life experiences."

DSD PILLARS
re·sil·ience

/DSD Authenticity

" the quality of being genuine or real; you're true to your own personality, values, and spirit. "

au·then·tic·i·ty

/DSD Empathy

" the ability to sense other people's emotions, coupled with the ability to imagine what someone else might be thinking or feeling. "

em·pa·thy

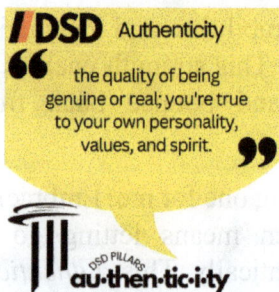

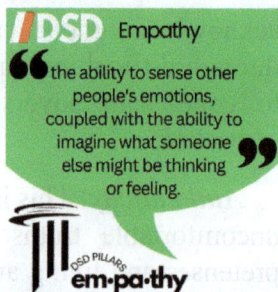

In summary, doing a *Deep Shallow Dive* and *Calling a Spade a Spade*, even when uncomfortable, is a transformative process that can strengthen you. It promotes *self-awareness*, *authenticity*, and *empathy* and makes you more resilient. It also empowers you to effect positive change in your life and society, ultimately leading to a more meaningful and fulfilling existence.

While the mindset may be challenging, the personal growth and transformation rewards are worth the effort. As we continue exploring uncomfortable truths through the *Deep Shallow Dive* process and the concept of *Calling a Spade a Spade*, I want you to join me on this road to self-discovery.

Through the pages of this book, I aim to provide direction, motivation, and thought-provoking insights that encourage you to embrace your uncomfortable truths, expand your mind, and ultimately lead a more authentic and fulfilling life. I will also be honest and raw with you.

This begins now, and the possibilities for personal growth and transformation are there if you let them. It's me and you. Let's do this.

At the end of several chapters, we will use the DSD methodology to frame what we learned and covered in that chapter.

Chapter End DSD:

GO DEEP:

Be truly honest with yourself throughout this process. It's private—only share with others if you choose to. At the end of each chapter, reflect deeply on what we've explored. I will prompt you, but you must be honest with yourself—painfully honest.

STAY SHALLOW:

I'll guide you on maintaining a *shallow* approach following our *deep* exploration. This might seem trivial, but it's crucial for making your *deep* insights practical and achievable. It's about turning your grand ideas into realistic, actionable steps, not just lofty dreams that never happen.

Staying *shallow* helped me do everything, including writing this book, which initially seemed daunting. But once I dove *deep* into what I wanted to talk about, I stayed *shallow* and broke it down into themes and chapters, and lo and behold, I saw it. I saw this book come together, and it did.

DIVE IN:

Lastly, to conclude each chapter, we'll focus on how you plan to *dive* in. Remember, without action, these are just words. It's about putting ideas into practice and making them a part of your reality.

People come
into your life
for a reason,
a season or
a lifetime...

Same as this
Book. I hope it plays
a role in your Life.

Chapter End Notes

Chapter 3:

YOU.
Your Personal Growth.

BE AUTHENTIC WITH YOURSELF.

Stay passionate.
Never stop loving what you do.

@DEEPSHALLOWDIVE

Chapter 3: YOU.
Your Personal Growth.

Deep Shallow Dive. Yes, I made up the term. I coined it to capture the essence of my explorations: diving into the heart of outwardly confusing and complicated matters to uncover *deeper* potential narratives while keeping them simple.

This deliberate oxymoron highlights my unique approach over the past four years, where I've explored and shared these narratives on Instagram, Facebook, and the Podcast. By embracing this juxtaposition, I have tried to explain the complexities of diverse situations and topics, offering a fresh, easy-to-understand perspective on historical and current events.

Building on my reflection we discussed in Chapter 1, once you truly begin to look within, a transformation unfolds, leading you down the path of personal growth and healing. This path is unique for everyone, but at its core, it involves expanding your understanding of yourself and your place in the world. This enables personal growth.

Personal Growth is about developing strengths, acquiring new skills, and improving your mindset. It's the process of becoming more resilient, confident, and effective in navigating life's challenges. It's like fine-tuning your inner radar to tackle your problems and pursue your goals more effectively.

A big part of personal growth recognizes that having questions is okay. When we were growing up, we would ask questions all the time. Why? Why? Why? I remember that line of questioning from my niece and nephew when they were four or five, and I'm sure I was the same at their age.

For many people, myself included, that inquisitive mind seemed to go into hibernation the more we started adulting, as they say. Honestly, before 2020, what was there even to question? But since then, the questions have begun to emerge. The questions caused my awakening, which led to more personal reflection and growth.

In this chapter, we'll explore the steps you can take to cultivate your growth, ensuring that you're not just moving through life but understanding it and evolving as you go. Continual personal growth can lead to a more fulfilling life. It can lead to better relationships because you can connect better with others when you know yourself better. It can also mean finding a more profound sense of purpose because your eyes are wide open about everything. You start to see more than what's inside the box once you realize there is a box.

The concept of *Deep Shallow Dive*, when applied to personal growth, provides a straightforward path to self-discovery. To put it simply, self-discovery means trying to understand yourself better. It's like looking inside yourself to figure out what you're good at, what you like, and what makes you... well, you. It's like being a detective about your feelings and thoughts. It helps you be in touch with them and honest with yourself. You are honest internally, even if you never share that with anyone else.

When you discover more about yourself, it can help you make better choices and be happier. It prompts you to deeply explore your experiences, emotions, and past events while keeping things clear and straightforward. To illustrate this, I have discovered something personal: I am sensitive about my friends' relationships with their parents, particularly their fathers. It's because I lost my dad in 2015, and that hit me harder than I ever expected.

Time has been a healer, giving me perspective on the 42 years I had with him. Those years were a gift, and not a day goes by that I don't wish for one more. So, I tell my friends, make the most of your time. Call your parents more often. Please try to be there for them and share in their lives, especially at this stage.

Help them with what you think is simple and that they should understand because we do, like technology. You can get frustrated; trust me, I know. But think about how many times they were frustrated with you growing up. Remember, they did not grow up with all this stuff; we did.

Get curious about their younger years—you'll be amazed to discover who they were before they were your mom and dad. They were just a guy and a girl—the same as us. And take photos—those moments are precious. Start to build a friendship with them, alongside the bond of family. In an instant, all you'll have are those memories. Because one day, poof. They are gone.

Luckily, I did all that with my Dad starting in 2004, so my last 11 years with him were different. He was still my Dad, but we were friends—good friends. In hindsight, I wish I had done even more, and I hope this personal share puts that on your radar, for whatever that's worth. I love you, Dad.

Back to *Personal Growth*. Embracing the DSD principles and balancing depth with simplicity makes your personal growth journey smoother and more effective. I've done it, and this book is the culmination of that work. Keeping everything simple when figuring yourself out comes down to a few handy tips. Again, go *deep*, stay *shallow*, *dive* in.

First tip:

Know what you want. Whether it's understanding something about yourself or reaching a goal, having a clear idea helps you stay on track without making things too complicated.

I know what I want. I want to make a more significant impact and be an encouraging voice. I knew I wanted to do more after seeing the positive engagement from my posts, stories, and podcasts. I want to do more because it helps people.

Therefore, I know what I want. I want to help people become more authentic with themselves. This book is part of that.

Second tip:

Remember to be nice to yourself as you try to accomplish what you want. Believe me when I say I'm my own harshest critic. I always need to be doing more in my mind. This is ongoing with me, and I have not solved it, but I have learned if you are patient and gentle during this effort, you'll stop being so hard on yourself and overthinking stuff.

For example, as soon as I decided to start the podcast or even write this book, I had to temper myself because I wanted to get more episodes recorded or get this book written so badly, so fast, that it frustrated me.

I was going *deep* but falling into the trap of overcomplicating things and not staying *shallow*, thus never diving in. I was not allowing my personal growth to happen because

I was focused on the results, not the journey. I stopped doing that, and it worked. It truly is about the journey.

This book is proof.

Third tip:

Strive for forward momentum. Forward momentum is the force that propels an object or an idea forward in a particular direction. In a figurative sense, like this book, it can also refer to the progress or advancement of a specific project or idea. Remember, the goal is to grow toward what we want to accomplish. To do that, keep moving forward, step by step, bit by bit, every day. Gain forward momentum.

Nothing significant happens overnight; this patient approach goes against our instant gratification world. Also, remember that mobile phones have created this culture of instant gratification, with all the apps and accessibility to things. This mentality created by our relationship with our phones causes an inherent challenge with personal growth.

Personal Growth takes time, and our mobile phones are distractions. In many ways, they save us time, which is excellent, but they also create that need for immediate gratification, extending into less inherently possible areas. Life today is geared not to take time but to be fast and immediate. But remember, having personal growth takes time, so afford yourself that time.

One tool to help with these tips is to incorporate the concept of joy into your day in any way you can.

Joy is just a feeling of pleasure or happiness. Joy can be big or small. Joy is an inner feeling. Believe it or not, I prefer small joy. I love to enjoy simple things daily. It's about living in the moment and not getting overwhelmed by too many thoughts or future worries.

Here's an example of a small joy: I love coffee. Like many others, I have coffee every morning. I genuinely get pleasure from having my morning coffee. It starts my day off happy because I love the taste. That first cup every morning brings me joy, especially that first sip.

My mom loves to walk. She wakes up daily and goes for a one-hour walk instead of having a coffee first thing. That starts her day off on the right foot, pun intended. She says it genuinely brings her joy and sets a nice tone for the rest of her day.

In short, to allow yourself to achieve *Personal Growth*, try to start every day with something that brings you joy. Think small. Start the day with that. Then, look for other small wins that bring you joy throughout your day. I am all about small wins— little things that make you happy.

Another tool is journaling, a great way to declutter your mind. Writing down your thoughts and feelings helps you sort through your emotions and understand what's happening.

I'll be honest: I don't journal in the old-school way of pen and paper. Instead, I use iPhone Notes, apps like Todoist and Notion, and even my Apple/Google Calendar. I capture so many things on my phone. It keeps me organized, and I feel more in control of my life when I am organized. In my calendar, I track everything from my meetings to social gatherings, workouts, car washes, and the Formula 1 race schedule.

This also applies to my health. I track my health in every way that I can. I track my sleep. I track the daily steps that I take, and I track my weight. They all go right into my Fitbit app.

This tracking helps me identify patterns and trends influencing my overall well-being. By analyzing this data, I make informed decisions about diet, exercise, and habits that could either boost my health or need improvement.

This constant monitoring is a motivational tool, encouraging me to maintain or elevate my commitment to a healthier lifestyle.

For example, I create a calendar event on my phone when measuring my blood pressure at home, CVS, or Walmart. I start the entry with keywords such as 'BP,' so if I need to find all my blood pressure results, I search 'BP' on my phone, and they are all listed.

Here is a screenshot so you can see this in action:

Actual Entries

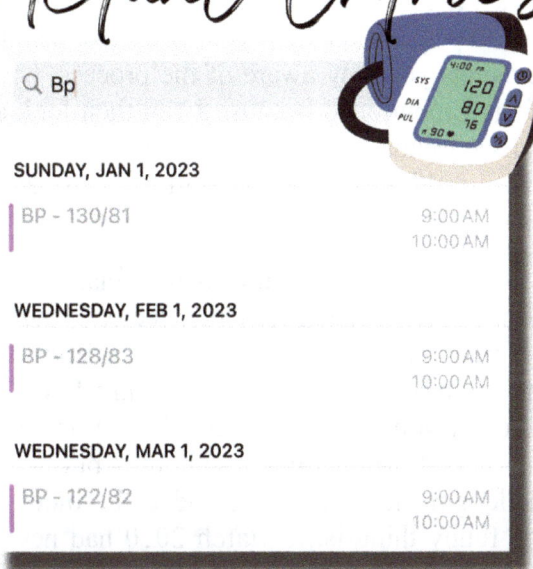

Q Bp

SUNDAY, JAN 1, 2023

BP - 130/81　　　　　　　　　　　9:00 AM
　　　　　　　　　　　　　　　　10:00 AM

WEDNESDAY, FEB 1, 2023

BP - 128/83　　　　　　　　　　　9:00 AM
　　　　　　　　　　　　　　　　10:00 AM

WEDNESDAY, MAR 1, 2023

BP - 122/82　　　　　　　　　　　9:00 AM
　　　　　　　　　　　　　　　　10:00 AM

I track all this to monitor my health and stay informed about my body. That mind/body connection is so powerful. When you understand and track your body and health, you are more connected with yourself, allowing *Personal Growth*.

It is also motivating, and we need that. Doing this could seem cumbersome, but I make it simple by tracking it right on my phone when it happens. It's easy, especially once it becomes a habit and you see the value. Try it. Start tracking more things using calendar events or notes on your phone.

Another tool is regular self-reflection. Self-reflection can help you maintain simplicity and clarity. It goes hand in hand with the tracking. Taking time to pause and assess your progress, insights, and goals lets you stay aware of the process. I track the things I mentioned because I can then look at them and see trends and patterns. It's like having life data on yourself, and once you start tracking and noting things, you feel more on top of your life.

Staying open-minded is also crucial for *Personal Growth*. Considering new perspectives and insights that may challenge your beliefs can lead to *deeper* understanding. Now, some #realtalk: I will not lie; the older you get, the harder this is. I never thought that would be the case with me, but it is. It is challenging to stay open-minded the older we get. The funny thing is, if March 2020 had never taken place, staying open-minded as I get older would have been even more challenging. But March 2020 did take place.

It did, and our world has been different since then, with all the various things that have occurred. It just has. But again, it also woke me up to other things, including embracing being open-minded. *Silver Linings Ray Book*. That one was a bit of a stretch, but I hope you get it!

Also, I hate to say this, but staying open-minded is more complicated because of good old social media. Social media has many promising applications and qualities but has created a culture of conflict. Many would even go so far as to say that social media is toxic, especially a platform like Twitter, now called X.com. It can be if you let it and engage in it that way.

For example:

Social Media Post: "I love apples! I just love them apples!"

Social Media Reaction: "What! Don't you love oranges? Or bananas? You are a fruit racist."

Hopefully, you are laughing because you get my point. Please don't engage in the negative on social media; it will not accomplish anything. Overall, try to stay open-minded about things because times have changed, and we must change with them.

Another great way to achieve *Personal Growth* is by engaging in creative outlets or anything that provides a simple and expressive way to explore and communicate your emotions. It's always possible to learn something new, and there are so many tools these days to help you that anyone can be creative. Creativity often leads to profound insights. It has brought me more of that small joy I discussed earlier.

Take your time with this. Whether you create a fun invitation for your next party using Canva or create a music playlist on your Spotify to play during that party, create. If you post creative images of the party on Instagram or take it up a notch and make helpful How-to videos on YouTube for others to learn from, create.

Whether you're cooking new recipes or learning new editing software like Capcut, you are always young enough to find a new creative outlet that you enjoy. Thanks to rapid technological advancements, we now have many tools to help us in various aspects of our lives. Whether you're using a phone, computer, or tablet, someone somewhere has developed an excellent solution to help make your life easier and more efficient. So, it's always worth exploring the options and finding the best tools. This is technology at its finest.

One quick note. Again, this stuff takes time. *Personal Growth* is more of a mentality, meaning, more than anything, it's you deciding that you are not done learning and growing. But when throwing yourself into new ventures, knowing when to take breaks and seek support prevents feeling overwhelmed and protects your emotional well-being. I'm guilty of this. I need to be better about taking breaks. I need to improve about letting myself recharge. Honestly, I am terrible at that and will strive to improve.

In summary, approaching your exploration into your *Personal Growth* with curiosity and a desire to learn keeps you engaged and motivated. Regularly reviewing your progress and revisiting your intentions helps maintain focus and clarity.

By incorporating these strategies into your exploration, you can strike a nice balance between diving into self-discovery and maintaining simplicity and clarity.

Chapter End DSD:

GO DEEP:

Pick something you want to learn, improve, or do. It can be anything, but let's pick something you feel is part of your *Personal Growth* and that you want to accomplish.

For example, do you want to start a podcast?

Do you want to learn how to start your podcast?

What is something you want to learn or get better at? Whatever it is, please write it down here in this space provided: (write it below)

Now, let's imagine learning to go *deep* with starting a podcast (or whatever you wrote above), which is like learning to grow a garden. When you start a garden, you first decide what you want to grow.

Is it flowers, vegetables, or maybe both? Starting a podcast is similar. You think about what you want to discuss—maybe stories, current affairs, or interviews with interesting people.

Next, just like choosing a spot for your garden where the sun shines and the soil is good, you pick a quiet place to record your podcast and get the right equipment, like a microphone and software.

Then, you start planting your seeds. For your podcast, that means recording your first episodes. Try different ways of talking and add music, just like you might try planting your seeds in various patterns or using other tools to help them grow.

You care for your garden by watering the plants and pulling out the weeds as it grows. With your podcast, you listen to your episodes and see what sounds good and what doesn't, like figuring out what's helping your garden and what's not.

I do this a lot.

I listen to myself a lot.

It's okay to laugh at that; I laughed while typing it.

Finally, when your vegetables and flowers are ready, you feel proud to share them with others. With your podcast, when you're happy with how your episodes sound, you share them on the internet for everyone to listen to, and you hope they enjoy listening to it as much as you enjoyed recording it.

That's going *deep* into starting your podcast. You learn and get better with each episode.

STAY SHALLOW:

Staying *shallow* in *Personal Growth* means keeping things simple and easy to manage. It's about focusing on the basics rather than getting lost in too many details. Think of it as learning to float in a swimming pool before trying to swim in the *deep* end. You're still in the water, learning to move and be comfortable without going too *deep* or fast. This way, you can enjoy the process and grow without the stress of thinking you will drown!

Learning to stay *shallow* with starting a podcast, like growing a garden, means trying to do only a little at a time. Instead of trying to grow every type of plant right away, start with just a few easy-to-care-for flowers or vegetables. This way, you get the hang of gardening basics—watering, sunlight, and soil—without worrying about the more complicated stuff, like fertilizers or pruning techniques.

In podcasting, staying *shallow* means starting with what you can comfortably handle. You could start by recording shorter episodes or sticking to topics you're already familiar with. You use simple recording tools instead of professional-grade equipment. Instead of creating the perfect podcast with many segments and sound effects, you focus on sharing your ideas clearly and having a good conversation with your listeners or guests.

In the garden, you enjoy watching your first plants grow and caring for them, while in podcasting, you enjoy making your first episodes and learning as you go. This approach keeps the process fun and manageable, and you can slowly add more complexity to your podcast as you become more comfortable, just like gradually expanding your garden over time.

DIVE IN:

Lastly, diving into *Personal Growth* is about taking action and immersing yourself in the experience. It's about getting your hands dirty with the soil, planting the seeds yourself, and caring for them daily. You're actively involved in the process, learning from doing and making adjustments based on that learning.

When starting a podcast, diving in means moving beyond planning and preparing to record and publish your episodes. It's about overcoming fears and doubts and sharing your voice with the world. You might start by setting a launch date for your podcast and committing to a schedule, like deciding to release a new episode every week.

You learn to edit, ask for feedback, and promote your podcast. With each step, you're actively engaged in growing your podcast, just like you tend to your garden daily and watch it flourish.

Diving in is committing to the growth process, taking tangible steps, and embracing the challenges as part of your growth. Good news for aspiring podcasters: I've shared my experience in an episode dedicated to how I launched the DSD podcast.

Scan the QR code below, and you'll be directed to our website. Or listen to this episode anywhere you listen to your podcasts; look for EP #5:

//DSD Podcast. EP#5: Launch Your Podcast:

Chapter End Notes

Chapter 4:

GO DEEP.
Seek Understanding.

Stay motivated.
Never stop reaching
for your
goals.

@DEEPSHALLOWDIVE

BE AUTHENTIC WITH YOURSELF.

Chapter 4: GO DEEP.
Seek Understanding.

Ok. It's time to understand going *deep* as it relates to understanding things. Have you ever paused to consider the profound impact of seeking *deep* understanding?

Let's return to March 2020; it marked a transformative era for me. It was then that I began to delve beneath the surface of things—examining the tumultuous world and the depths of my thought processes. In this chapter, we'll explore the transformative mindset that emerges when you embark on the path to *deeper* understanding in all facets of your life.

The quest for seeking *deep* understanding isn't just beneficial; it's a cornerstone of personal development. My transformation has revealed that proper understanding offers us unparalleled insight, setting the stage for decisions that stand firm without a trace of doubt.

Why should seeking *deep* understanding be at the top of your list?

It's simple: it does wonders for expanding your mind and sharpening your critical thinking. Imagine bringing light to a room that's been shrouded in shadows. It's not just illumination; it's a complete shift in how you perceive your surroundings. The room now could look larger and nicer. Or, you may realize you just added more work to your plate, as the room may need a coat of paint or a new carpet.

Moreover, such depth in understanding fuels informed decision-making. March 2020 was a turning point for me, underscoring the need to push past simple answers and posturing truths. This chapter embodies that shift, a pivot towards a more nuanced approach to dissecting and grasping the world around us.

This also started my shift. In the pursuit of personal growth, skimming the surface won't cut it. A profound understanding propels you into the depths where accuracy and full-bodied knowledge lead to decisions that are not just informed but wise. That's the kind of insight I'm eager for you to gain and possess.

But the importance of seeking understanding stretches beyond enhancing critical thinking—it's fundamental to solving problems and making decisions with clarity and conviction. It's the spark that ignites your intellectual curiosity.

Moreover, seeking *deep* understanding is critical to making meaningful choices. A robust understanding of any topic allows you to thoughtfully balance pros and cons, foresee outcomes, and confidently select the most fitting path forward.

But wait, there's more. Seeking *deep* understanding nurtures one of the core pillars we've discussed: *empathy*. It invites us to step into others' shoes, fostering *deeper* relationships, effective communication, and a profound sense of connection. Practicing *empathy* has been transformative for me, and it is as straightforward as exchanging perspectives.

Here is how I practice *empathy*: I do a role reversal. I put myself in their position and put them in mine. I promise you that you will understand *empathy* that way. Just put yourself in their shoes and then put them in yours.

We seek *deeper* understanding because it gives us the knowledge and insights to unravel complex issues. Today's world often only shows us the surface, yet the challenges lie beneath that. We are headline-driven, but headlines can be deceptive. By venturing beyond the headline, we can identify the underlying causes of problems and forge enduring solutions.

This pursuit of depth fosters personal growth and enhances another DSD pillar: *self-awareness*. Remember, it all starts with *self-awareness*, and seeking understanding helps you know your inner character and makes you think. As we delve into the depths, we uncover our biases and thought patterns, equipping us to evaluate them through this fresh perspective we're fostering. It takes us off autopilot.

An underestimated aspect of seeking *deeper* understanding is its profound effect on resolving conflicts. When we seek to comprehend all sides of the story, it becomes a powerful tool for reconciliation. It again allows us to empathize, find common ground, and engage in dialogue that builds bridges rather than walls.

The role reversal technique mentioned earlier is crucial here, as it fosters understanding and helps bring about resolutions. Setting aside our feelings can also provide the space to approach matters with a cool head. When you tap into your *empathy*, you can control your emotions.

In the current climate of information overload and the rampant spread of misinformation, a *deep* understanding is also a defense against deception. As artificial intelligence continues to evolve, the need for this critical analysis becomes ever more pressing. Being able to distinguish between reliable information and falsehoods is like having a superpower in an age dominated by algorithms. Our common sense is the ace up our sleeve in this battle of wits. Do not underestimate your common sense and gut instinct simply because technology has advanced.

Additionally, a profound understanding reveals how interconnected factors within a system or issue can be. It's about stepping back to see the larger design, the intricate web of cause and effect.

Elevating our vantage point to a bird's-eye view not only allows us to see the whole picture but also to anticipate future moves and ask the tough questions:

Why is someone doing something?

What's their angle?

What do they have to gain?

What do they have to lose?

Who benefits?

Who loses?

We need to embrace these questions and not be scared to ask them. This does not make you a pessimist or a negative person. This will make you a more informed person who feels more confident.

Remember, when you go through this process with something, you do not need to broadcast it to the world or share it on social media. It's just a tool to help you. Topical knowledge may provide short-term solutions, but profound understanding leads to lasting and sustainable change. It equips us with the insights and strategies to address root causes and create enduring solutions.

Lastly, seeking *deep* understanding embraces complexity. It acknowledges that life is multifaceted and only sometimes has straightforward solutions. By embracing complexity, we can navigate the intricacies of the world with clarity and wisdom.

Seeking *deep* understanding is the backbone of a *Deep Shallow Dive*.

In summary, seeking *deep* understanding goes beyond the surface and enriches our knowledge, mindset, and decision-making abilities. It enhances critical thinking, *empathy*, and problem-solving skills, contributing to personal growth, effective communication, and the meaningful ability to address complex issues. Seeking *deep* understanding empowers individuals to navigate an increasingly complex world with clarity and insight.

Ok, but how about a real-world example?

What does seeking *deep* understanding look like?

What does it mean to understand something big and complicated?

Allow me to illustrate this using an event that profoundly moved me. On October 7, 2023, when the situation erupted in the Gaza Strip within Israel, it was not just another headline; it became a catalyst for my *deep dive* into the complicated history of the region.

I wanted to seek a profound understanding of that situation for my benefit and knowledge base.

Determined to understand that region's history beyond the surface, I immersed myself in the chronicles of the conflicts and the peace efforts, the narratives of people on both sides, and the geopolitical intricacies that have shaped the current state of affairs. This was not a mere theoretical exercise but a rational and poignant analysis that took me through the layers of historical context, personal stories of strife and *resilience*, and the complex web of international relations.

At the same time, the crisis was playing out in real-time across social media. My understanding grew profoundly as I sought to make sense of the events.

This allowed me to view this situation and global conflicts with a keener perspective, fostering *empathy* and a *deeper* appreciation for the intricate dance of the various forces at play.

The more I learned, the more I saw that this wasn't just about people arguing about what happened that day. It was about the land, the history, the religions, the homes, the families, and how everyone had a different story about what was fair. It was about the past and the future. The present was about the past and the future.

I learned that to understand something, you have to listen to all sides and especially consider how the past shapes the present. Global geopolitics is like chess, so I started analyzing past moves to try and understand the present ones and even try to predict the upcoming moves, although the latter proved more difficult.

I immersed myself in radio interviews, reading articles, and finding old footage from 1948 and even back to 1917. I worked to understand the history of both sides of this conflict. By doing that, I could understand the backstory and explain it to others in a way that helps them understand this complex situation.

The more I learned, the broader my perspective grew. I could better appreciate the multiple dimensions of the conflict, seeing beyond my presumptions to the heart of a genuinely political saga. This research didn't just educate me; it transformed my worldview. It did that for many people, as it played out on social media.

To truly understand such a sensitive issue, one must listen with *empathy*, analyze carefully, and accept the discomfort of no easy solutions. Embracing this multifaceted approach has sharpened my investigative skills and heightened my emotional intelligence, laying the groundwork for *deeper* understanding.

I took this approach into my life and found myself better equipped to tackle complex challenges with a balanced view and a thoughtful approach. This situation in Gaza also evoked many of the seeds I planted with you earlier:

Resilience: I made myself face the uncomfortable truths I saw, which was emotionally challenging. I looked at the images. I watched the videos. Yes, this wasn't easy at times, but I did it. It helped build my *resilience*.

Authenticity: This remains a big one for me. Embracing uncomfortable truths often can make you pessimistic, but only if you let it. Don't let it. Being authentic to me means accepting the truth, whether it's good or bad.

Self-Awareness: Recognizing uncomfortable truths about societal issues can lead to a desire to become more aware of one's feelings. It did with me. It also made me want to *Call a Spade a Spade*.

Uncomfortable truths often bring fear and anxiety. Especially in today's cancel culture mentality, you may be scared to say what you mean. Don't be. The truth truly does set you free as long as you are fair. Just be fair.

If you are fair, no one can poke a hole in what you are saying. This is also part of *calling a Spade a Spade*. But this is easier when you don't have skin in the game or a dog in the fight and can call balls and strikes. Wow, that was a montage of expressions.

Once again, the most important of all is e*mpathy*. I embraced it and let it guide me. From *empathy* for the families of the hostages to *empathy* for the innocent civilians caught in this geopolitical struggle, doing that role reversal in both cases allowed me to understand and empathize with all the innocent bystanders.

Those interested in learning about that situation from a DSD standpoint can scan the QR code below, and you'll be directed to the start of this 9-Part Series on our website. You can also listen anywhere you listen to your podcasts; go to the *Deep Shallow Dive* Podcast, scroll down, and start with Episode #34:

//DSD EP#34: The Holy Land Saga: Israel vs. Palestine - Part 1:

Trust me on this: seeking *deep* understanding is a transformative process that leads to personal growth, self-discovery, and a *deeper* connection with the world around us. By delving beyond surface-level information, embracing vulnerability, and cultivating mindfulness, you get to know yourself better and embark on a mission of profound meaning. Through this mission, you can truly understand yourself and navigate the complexities of life with *authenticity* and integrity.

Again, remember why it is essential to go beyond surface-level information and seek *deep* understanding. The answer lies in the multitude of benefits that come with going *deeper*. Going *deeper* provides more data, enabling informed decision-making and critical thinking, and helps you get to the correct data.

Going *deeper* with common sense fosters *empathy*, problem-solving, and innovation. It leads to personal growth and facilitates conflict resolution. This will be needed with AI's continued acceleration, as it prevents falling for misinformation and seeing the narratives as they play out. Just lean on your common sense. Get back in tune with your thoughts and feelings.

Knowing yourself and understanding your thoughts and feelings can change you significantly. It's like going on an adventure inside your mind. This mindset helps you grow your knowledge, become more aware of who you are, and make better choices. It sharpens your radar.

Life's puzzles become more accessible as we get better at them. We see things more clearly and make decisions with confidence. It's about getting to the heart of who we are and learning to move through the world with a sense of our depth and purpose.

Chapter End DSD:

GO DEEP:

As we did in the last chapter, now pick something you want to seek a *deeper* understanding of. Again, it can be anything, but let's pick something that has always been confusing or complicated.

For example, do you want to try Intermittent Fasting to lose weight?

Whatever it is, write it down here:

Let's think about the heart of the matter. Like unraveling the complex history of the Israel-Palestine conflict, a *deep dive* can transform your understanding, helping you uncover biases and embrace *empathy*.

Let's use Intermittent Fasting to help you think through what you wrote above. To go *deep*, you start by researching the methodology behind Intermittent

Fasting. You learn about the different methods, like the 16/8 method, where you fast for 16 hours and eat during an 8-hour window, or the 5:2 method, where five days a week are routine eating days, while the other two restrict calories to 500–600 per day.

You read studies on how Intermittent Fasting affects the body, such as changes in hormone levels, cell repair processes, and potential benefits for brain health. You look into how it might influence weight loss, energy levels, and long-term wellness. You even talk to friends who may have tried it to get their perspective.

By examining all this information, you're not just following a trend but building a *deep* understanding of how and why Intermittent Fasting works. This knowledge helps you make informed choices about whether Intermittent Fasting suits you and how to implement it in a way that aligns with your body's needs and lifestyle.

The DSD methodology for Intermittent Fasting equips you with insights to approach this health strategy thoughtfully and effectively.

Research: Read, watch, or listen to people who resonate with you and you trust.

Talk with Friends: Discussing with others can open new perspectives, like trading stories around a campfire.

Understand the Choices: Think about the pros and cons of each and how they align with your values and goals. This is about making sense of your options rather than just identifying them.

Decide which Route to Take: Finally, choose your path forward with intention, like choosing which route to take when your navigation gives you choices. Make a decision that feels right for you. It's about committing to a direction with the clarity and confidence you've gained through this process.

STAY SHALLOW:

Staying *shallow* when seeking *deep* understanding about what you wrote down again is meant to keep the exploration manageable. While it's essential to seek depth, stay aware of the minutiae. Stay focused on key insights that drive understanding forward. It's about maintaining a clear view from a 30,000-foot perspective, ensuring you see the bigger picture without getting bogged down by every detail.

With Intermittent Fasting, staying *shallow* can be picking one timeframe.

I recommend the 16/8—not eating for 16 hours from, let's say, 7 PM to 11 AM, then eating generally from 11 AM to 7 PM daily. Skip breakfast and eat your first meal at 11 AM, then finish dinner by 7 PM.

You keep it straightforward and pay attention to how you feel: Are you super hungry? Are you energized? Are you tired? Or is it easy?

This approach allows you to adapt Intermittent Fasting to your life without feeling overwhelmed by the complexity of its underlying science.

Staying *shallow* with Intermittent Fasting means dipping your toes into the practice, observing the immediate effects on your day-to-day life, and deciding if it's a sustainable approach without getting bogged down by the broader implications and depth of information available.

DIVE IN:

Lastly, diving in when seeking *deep* understanding means immersing yourself in the learning process. Engage with challenging material, confront uncomfortable truths, and allow *empathy* to guide you. Your active participation in seeking *deep* understanding, like my dedication to learning about a global conflict, leads to personal growth and a more nuanced view of the world.

Diving into Intermittent Fasting means practicing your knowledge and starting the fasting regimen. You choose a method that suits your lifestyle—like the 16/8 method—and commit to it.

You're setting a schedule for when you'll eat and fast and sticking to it every day. I even set up

Calendar Events to pop up daily at 11 AM saying GO EAT and then at 7 PM saying STOP EATING!

I initially even had my smart speakers say that out loud, but after the second day, I realized that was no longer funny and pretty annoying, so I turned off that routine. That's called trial and error.

As part of *Diving In*, you're also keeping a journal to track your progress, noting how you feel, what you eat during your eating window, and any changes in your weight or energy levels. I did this again on my phone.

You're fully engaged with the process, making adjustments as needed based on your experiences. During your eating window, you might experiment with different foods to see how they affect your fasting and overall well-being. I went all protein and no carbs for a week to see if it made a difference. It did.

And weigh yourself. Track it.

In this active phase, you're not just thinking about Intermittent Fasting; you're living it. You're taking the initiative to see how this health strategy works for you and learning firsthand about its benefits and challenges.

This hands-on approach is the essence of *Diving In*—immersing yourself in the experience to understand and integrate it into your life.

Good news for any aspiring Intermittent Fasters. I did a comprehensive episode on my podcast that you can use in your research. Scan the QR code below, or you can also listen anywhere you listen to your podcasts:

//DSD Podcast. EP#74: Intermittent Fasting:

SCAN ME

EP#74 | Intermittent Fasting:

www.deepshallowdive.com

Available on All Platforms!

Chapter End Notes

BE AUTHENTIC WITH YOURSELF.

Chapter 5:

STAY SHALLOW.
Embrace Simplicity.

Stay hopeful.
Never stop believing in what's possible.

@DEEPSHALLOWDIVE

Chapter 5: STAY SHALLOW.
Embrace Simplicity.

The next topic is simple. I'm just kidding. Unfortunately, it should be, but it is not. In our fast-paced and complex world, embracing simplicity can often seem elusive. The distractions of modern life can hinder our ability to find clarity, focus, and inner peace. Is there ever a free moment anymore?

Maintaining a sense of simplicity and clarity is challenging. Digital excess, social media, information overload, consumer culture, work-life imbalance, multitasking, and entertainment and media consumption are just a few of the distractions that can pull us away from a simpler and more fulfilling life.

The constant stream of information on social media and the pressures of that culture makes it easy to get caught up in the chaos and hard to stop. But what if we could embrace simplicity and declutter our minds and lives to enhance our well-being? This chapter will explore practical steps to simplify our lives and their profound impact on our personal growth and overall welfare.

The problem, more than anything, is our phones. Even more than computers, what is it with these phones? They have changed the way we conduct our lives and manage our day. Don't get me wrong, a lot of good has come from them. But they have also cut into having quality time and being present in the moment. More on that later.

We can adopt various strategies to declutter our minds and simplify our lives. Mindfulness can help calm the mind, reduce stress, and improve focus. Mindfulness is the practice of being fully present and engaged at the moment, aware of your thoughts and feelings without judgment.

I practice it when I have that first cup of coffee every morning that brings me that small joy: the aroma of the coffee as I put the grounds into my coffee maker, the way the hot mug feels in my hand, the smell of the fresh brew, and then the taste.

I love the taste. I savor that first sip and am mindful about enjoying it.

Next, this one will be difficult and something we can tackle in steps. Taking a digital detox by setting aside specific times to disconnect from social media and your devices can also be beneficial. Social media is more straightforward to disconnect from because you can spend less time on the apps.

Regarding your phone, I started with not needing to have my phone next to me when watching TV. I set it across the room, as I found myself constantly fiddling with it while I was supposed to enjoy a series I binge-watch or my Formula 1 races that I love.

That simple action with my phone made me feel better and get back to enjoying what's on TV. This attachment to our phones has only been the past ten years since they became smartphones and allowed us to do so much more on them than before.

I also stopped taking my phone into the bathroom with me. I'm talking about the bathrooms in my own house! Do you do that? If not, good for you. If yes, again, thank you. Why do we do that? Notice I said we! Seriously. Why do we need to look at our phones when we are on the potty of all places?

It could be because it has become second nature to have our phones in our hands all the time, but when we start to embrace the simplicity of life, we can begin to take back certain bad habits like that. I am trying to do that. I can't believe I put that in print, but I promised to keep honest and raw in this book. That's how we grow and get better.

Ok, we are moving on. Insert the collective sigh of relief!

So, what does starting on the path to embracing simplicity look like?

It looks like pausing to consider what ignites your passion and what deserves a spot in your life. I love that phrase: *what deserves a spot in your life*? It's about identifying the things that resonate with you and the things that, well, quite frankly, do not.

Embracing simplicity means consciously choosing where to invest your time and energy, ensuring they flow towards activities that fill your cup to the brim. Realize this needs to be unique to you. There are areas and parts you will share with your family, friends, kids, parents, and others. But there are parts of embracing simplicity that must be all about you and what makes you happy.

For example, embracing simplicity can involve decluttering your home or office environment. Decluttering has gained popularity since COVID-19, and a minimalist view of things has emerged over the last few years. That was due to all our time at home, and we realized how cluttered those areas had become.

It could also be due to the new sleek design of furniture or home products, but I see more and more people trying to simplify their kitchens, garages, and homes. This approach can also filter into your mindset and have a positive impact.

Decluttering isn't merely about organization; it's about designing a space that echoes the tranquility of a clear mind. Adopting minimalism is more than a style choice; it's a commitment to quality over quantity. It also just feels clean. Clean and nice.

It's letting go to bring in more joy, clarity, and experiences that touch your soul. When we pare down to the essentials, we don't just create room in our closets; we create space in our lives for growth, happiness, and an abundance of what we love.

Speaking of closets, here is another personal example I want to share. I simplified my wardrobe. I'm not just talking about giving away some clothes I do not wear anymore, although I do that regularly. But I realized that I like wearing only three or four colors for the most part: white, black, grey, and navy. So, I stopped buying clothes in other colors since I knew I would never wear them. I embraced simplicity with my clothes via colors.

Simplifying my wardrobe was like clearing the fog from a cloudy morning. It wasn't just about having fewer clothes; it was about choosing to surround myself with pieces that resonated with who I am and how I wanted to present myself to the world. This decluttering of my closet also turned out to be a decluttering of my mind. With fewer choices, my mornings became simpler.

Here's what I did: I started by pulling out every item I owned and asking myself:

Does wearing this item bring me joy?

Does it make me feel confident when I wear it?

Do I enjoy wearing it?

Have I worn it in the past three years?

I know that seems like a long time, but if you go right now and look in your closet, I bet at least 50% of what is in there, you cannot even remember the last time you wore it. If you want to get a laugh, feel free to step away from reading and do that!

After going through way too many dress shirts and pants and even suits, if that answer was 'no,' then it didn't earn its spot in my life. I gave away or donated the clothes that no longer served me, keeping only the ones that fit well, looked good, and made me feel great. This wasn't a one-time purge; it has become a mindful practice.

More important, though, was that mindset about my wardrobe moving forward. Whenever I consider buying new clothes, I think about the place that item has in my life and its impact on my clarity of mind. It's not 'just less is more'—it's about more of what matters. More of what I like. It's more of what I will wear versus residing in my closet for another three (3) years.

By embracing simplicity in my wardrobe, I've found that I'm saving time, reducing stress, and making more intentional and sustainable choices. This shift has brought unexpected peace and an empowering sense of self-expression.

Embracing simplicity also contributes significantly to personal growth and overall well-being. Reducing stress and anxiety and increasing focus and clarity can enhance appreciation and gratitude. If we let it, embracing simplicity can touch almost every aspect of our lives.

We can find more small daily things that bring joy to our lives through simplicity. When those small daily things add up, you are happier. This really can happen, sometimes even without you realizing it.

Now, let me get back to talking about these digital devices. Have you ever felt like your digital devices own you more than you own them?

Embracing simplicity could mean disconnecting and finding that quiet time away from the pings and notifications. It's not about losing touch; it's about gaining touch with what's real—your real life, authentic connections, and the real moments of joy.

I'm aware that this isn't easy, and more than anything, I hope you become keenly aware of the sway your digital devices may hold over your life. We will reclaim that control, tipping the balance of power back into our hands—a subtle play on words intended.

Now, let's talk about our most precious commodity—our time. Managing it isn't about squeezing in more; it's about savoring what we choose to do. Embracing simplicity in our personal lives has become more pertinent than ever, especially considering the solitude many have encountered in recent years. While the increased time alone seemed daunting initially, it has also offered a unique opportunity to rediscover your passions and the activities that bring you joy.

When we simplify our lives, we peel away the non-essentials that have long cluttered our days and thoughts. We are left with space that can be filled not with just new things but new things that matter. This could be pursuing a long-neglected hobby, investing time learning a new skill, or simply indulging in the luxury of stillness and reflection.

Here's the beautiful part: In calm simplicity, we often find a fountain of pleasure, both small and big. Activities we love and have put aside for some time can now take center stage. Perhaps you've found solace in painting, comfort in writing, or joy in gardening—whatever your passion, simplicity gives you the time and the mental clarity to embrace it. For me, it led to starting the podcast, which led to writing this book.

As we continue to embrace simplicity in our personal lives, we give ourselves the priceless gift of time—time that can be spent on what makes us happiest, which enriches our souls and recharges our spirits.

Embracing simplicity is not about having less; it's about making room for more—more joy, more peace, more moments of being present. It's a process of shedding the excess to uncover what makes you happy.

Let's start this process together, and I will begin by walking the walk and making this chapter shorter than the previous ones as I again embrace simplicity.

Chapter End DSD:

GO DEEP:

As we did in the last chapter, pick something you want to embrace simplicity with. Pick something complicated in your life.

Here is one for me: *Sunday Night Meal Prep.*

Whatever it is, write it down here:

Let's go *deep* with meal prep. For me, that means a high-protein/low-carb diet and involves a strategic and thoughtful approach.

Here's a guide to getting started:

Understand Your Nutritional Targets:

Begin by understanding what *high-protein* and *low-carb* mean for your body. Determine your daily protein needs based on weight, activity level, and health goals. Learn which foods are high in protein— lean meats, fish, eggs, dairy products, legumes, and nuts—and which low-carb vegetables and fruits align with your diet.

Educate Yourself on Food Choices:

Educate yourself on the carbs to avoid or limit, like simple sugars, grains, and starch-heavy vegetables. Instead, focus on foods like leafy greens, berries, and high-fiber, non-starchy vegetables. Understand the role of fats in your diet and select healthy fats from sources like avocados, olive oil, and seeds.

Plan Your Meals:

Balance protein, fats, and low-carb vegetables in your meals. Sketch a weekly menu, ensuring each meal meets your dietary targets. For breakfast, consider omelets with vegetables and cheese; for lunch, consider salads with grilled chicken or fish; and prepare stir-fried or roasted meats and vegetables for dinner.

Supplement Wisely:

If you find it challenging to meet your protein requirements through food alone, consider a high-quality protein supplement, like a whey isolate or a plant-based protein powder. However, always aim to get most of your nutrients from whole foods.

Also, when it comes to your daily vitamins, think about taking a liquid version. One significant advantage of liquid vitamins is improved absorption.

Liquid vitamins do not have to go through the digestive process like pill form. Therefore, your body absorbs more nutrients, which get into your bloodstream faster.

Stay Hydrated:

High-protein diets can be dehydrating, so increase your water intake. Carry a water bottle and, if needed, set phone reminders or calendar events to drink water regularly throughout the day.

Going *deep* into the planning and preparation phase, you'll be able to stick to your high-protein/low-carb diet more efficiently, make informed choices, and set yourself up for success in achieving your health and fitness goals.

STAY SHALLOW:

I'm not going to lie; at least for me, meal prep inherently is a pain! To stay *shallow* and keep it simple, I simplify the process by choosing a small number of recipes that I know are healthy but easy to make and that I enjoy.

I rotate these meals throughout the week to reduce the number of eating decisions I have to make. This may sound boring, but you have to pick your battles.

Feeling healthy and good makes it worth that tradeoff. Here are some straightforward tips to keep meal prep easy and uncomplicated:

Use Simple Recipes:

Choose recipes with only a few ingredients and simple cooking methods. Grilled meats, steamed veggies, and salads are quick to prepare. Avoid recipes that require complex steps or uncommon ingredients.

Repeat Meals:

Feel free to eat the same thing several times a week. Find a couple of meals you enjoy and make them in bulk. This reduces the number of ingredients you need and simplifies shopping and cooking.

Cook One-Pot Meals:

One-pot meals can be a huge time-saver. They require less active cooking time and fewer dishes to clean afterward. Think about stews, casseroles, or stir-fries that combine protein and low-carb vegetables.

Raw and Ready-to-Eat:

Incorporate raw foods that don't require cooking. Snack on nuts, cheese, cold cuts, raw veggies, and salads. They are great for saving time and can be portioned out for the week in minutes.

Pre-Cut Vegetables:

Buy pre-cut vegetables or use a food processor to reduce prep time. Though they may be more expensive, the time saved can be worth the cost.

Rotisserie Chicken:

A rotisserie chicken from the grocery store can be a lifesaver. It's versatile, can be used for several meals, and saves cooking time. You know what I'm talking about if you are a Costco member.

Canned and Frozen Foods:

Utilize canned fish (like tuna or salmon) and frozen vegetables. They are quick to prepare, and frozen veggies are often pre-chopped and ready to cook. For the record, I do prefer non-frozen veggies, but again, pick your battles.

Cook in Bulk:

Choose one day to cook in bulk and make enough protein to last through the week. Grilled chicken, hard-boiled eggs, and baked fish can be cooked in large quantities and used in various ways throughout the week.

Smart Storage:

Invest in quality storage containers that make it easy to grab your meal and go.

Clear containers can help you see what's inside, making it easier to pick your meal quickly.

Keep Snacks Handy:

Have a selection of protein-rich, low-carb snacks ready to go.

Cheese sticks, yogurt, nuts, and boiled eggs are easy to grab without prep time.

Following these *stay shallow* strategies can streamline your meal prep process, making it more doable and less time-consuming while still sticking to your diet goals.

DIVE IN:

Trust me, it gets easier every time you do it, but when it comes to meal prep, you must allocate the time and do it. This means equipping yourself with the right tools and committing to the process.

Here's how you can do it.

Invest in Quality Kitchen Tools:

A larger air fryer can cook bigger batches of food, saving time and energy. You can quickly prepare high-protein items like chicken breasts, fish fillets, or even hard-boiled eggs without much fuss.

A food processor simplifies chopping, dicing, and slicing, making it efficient to prepare vegetables for salads, stir-fries, or snack packs.

A high-powered blender is perfect for making protein shakes, low-carb soups, or even grinding nuts and seeds.

Set a Regular Meal Prep Schedule:

Choose a day and time each week to dedicate to meal prepping. I do this on Sunday afternoon. Make it a non-negotiable routine, just like walking or your gym session.

Plan Your Menu:

Before your scheduled prep day, decide on the menu for the week. Balance variety and simplicity to ensure you're not overwhelmed, but enjoy your meals.

Shop Intentionally:

With your menu planned, create a shopping list and stick to it. Avoid impulse buys, especially items that don't fit your high-protein/low-carb plan.

Batch Cook and Portion:

Using your air fryer, oven, and stovetop, cook your protein sources in batches. At the same time, use your food processor to prepare your veggies. Portion your cooked food into meal-sized containers. Include a variety of proteins and veggies so you don't get bored.

Label Everything:

Label your containers with the date and contents. This will help you keep track of freshness and make it easy to grab the proper meal.

Prep Snacks:

Use your blender to make protein shakes in advance, and store them in the fridge for a quick grab-and-go snack. Prepare zip-lock bags with nuts, seeds, or cheese for a quick protein boost.

Embrace Efficiency:

Look for ways to multitask. While your air fryer works on the chicken, you could boil eggs on the stove or chop vegetables with the food processor. This way, you're using your time and kitchen appliances to their fullest potential.

Stay Committed:

Even on days when meal prepping feels like a chore, remember why you started. Stay focused on your health and wellness goals, and remember that each meal prep session is an investment in your future self.

By diving into meal prepping with the right mindset and tools, you'll make it a sustainable part of your healthy lifestyle, ensuring that nutritious meals are readily available even when life gets busy. I promise it gets easier each time!

QUICK NOTE:

In full disclosure, in 2013, after struggling for years with getting nauseous from pill form and getting them constantly stuck in my throat, I invented a liquid vitamin product called BUICED (pronounced boost). Our liquid products are better absorbed into your bloodstream vs. pill form or gummies.

Drinking your vitamins is like drinking coffee or a glass of wine. Caffeine and alcohol are more readily absorbed into your bloodstream as liquids. The same concept applies to our BUICED liquid vitamins.

BUICED.com offers our premium liquid vitamins. Visit us to learn more about our commitment to transparency, education, and quality in health and wellness.

Scan the QR code below, and you'll be directed straight to the BUICED.com website:

Chapter End Notes

BE AUTHENTIC WITH YOURSELF.

Chapter 6:

DIVE IN.
Go Deep + Staying Shallow.

Stay driven.
Never stop gaining forward momentum.

@DEEPSHALLOWDIVE

Chapter 6: DIVE IN.
Go Deep while Staying Shallow.

The concepts of seeking understanding and embracing simplicity represent the *deep* and the *shallow*, so we *dive* in when we combine these. As we begin Chapter 6, let's first revisit the four foundational pillars of the *Deep Shallow Dive* (DSD) methodology we discussed.

These pillars—*self-awareness*, *resilience*, *authenticity*, and *empathy*—are not abstract concepts but vital forces that propel us toward a life of purpose and meaning. We will explore them in depth.

While we explore how to balance the *deep dive* of seeking understanding with the clear waters of embracing simplicity, let's keep these pillars in mind. These pillars of DSD are all about cultivating our integrity. They remind us to stay true to who we are, to find strength even when obstacles test our resolve, and to nurture a spirit of understanding that stretches beyond our own experiences to embrace the hearts and minds of others. I think about them when diving into any topic and figuring it out.

As we embark on the subsequent sections of this book, we will shift gears to talk about a specific area of our lives and how we can apply the DSD methodology, apply *calling a Spade a Spade*, and apply these pillars to help us navigate each section and get better at that topic. By having our *Deep*

Shallow Dive approach and using these pillars as anchors for our emotions, I hope they provide you with a framework to handle life events better and more confidently. I use these myself as well.

Once you start contemplating and self-reflecting, you may discover you have a *deeper* core than you realized. Tapping into that brings self-awareness, leading to a more genuine version of yourself. That's what we're tackling here. That's the goal of all this.

The goal is to welcome moments that aren't always Instagram-ready per se but incredibly genuine. Embracing these aspects of our lives adds depth and purpose, making everything feel more meaningful and down-to-earth.

Let's start with *self-awareness* because it all starts there. Think of *self-awareness* as your inner GPS. Getting more self-aware can be as simple as pausing a beat to check in with yourself. When reacting to something, take a second to ask:

What's bugging me here?

Or do a quick review of the situation:

What made me feel good, and what didn't?

It's about noticing your patterns and feelings, like being an investigator in your own life.

Let's talk about getting honest and vulnerable with how we feel. Being vulnerable isn't about throwing your emotions out there without a care. It's about having the guts to be honest, even if it's scary or awkward.

When was the last time you let down your guard and let someone see the real you?

That stuff is golden.

And here's the thing about bringing *self-awareness* and vulnerability into your everyday life: It's not that hard. It's about being all in, in that moment. This also goes back to finding those small joys daily that I have harped on. Looking for small joys to make you happy helps you be in the moment and enjoy that part of your day to the fullest. That positive feeling is like the residual effect they say lifting weights has on burning calories after your workout; it will continue even after the workout.

Also, the concept of role reversal, which we discussed as it relates to empathy, can be used here with *self-awareness* and vulnerability. If a situation is emotional or sensitive, swap the roles and positions. You will find that putting yourself in the other person's shoes and looking at it that way helps you see their side. It makes you self-aware and vulnerable. I have become good at this and have tried to help those close to me with this technique.

The next pillar is *resilience*. Building *resilience* is also a lot like working out. Just like lifting weights, Pilates, or yoga can make you stronger, tackling life's daily challenges builds your *resilience*. So, when you're faced with a tough choice or a setback, don't step down—step up.

It's like learning to play Pickleball; it might be easy at first, but soon, you'll twist your ankle or develop plantar fasciitis. We are at about the halfway point of this book, and I threw that in there to see if you are paying attention—and get a laugh!

Okay. Next up is one of my favorite character traits: *authenticity*. *Authenticity* is about letting the real you come through without the filters. It's like being the same person on the outside that you are on the inside, even if that means showing your goofy laugh or admitting you're a nerd about something.

Embrace who you are, quirks and all, because the world needs more of this genuine version of you. I love authentic people. People who are themselves. I strive to be that.

The last pillar of DSD that we will use and try to cultivate is *empathy*. *Empathy* is putting yourself in someone else's shoes. It's about listening and understanding their position, even if you've never walked their path. As we discussed before, *empathy* goes hand in hand with the concept of doing a role reversal so that you can look at everything from their side.

By tuning in to others' feelings and perspectives, you're not just hearing them out; you're connecting on a human level that says: *I get where you're coming from*. *Empathy* has come into my life hand in hand with the *Deep Shallow Dive* methodology.

It has been triggered by all the events that have taken place, which have shaken me to my core. I'm different. I've changed for the better because I am more aware of other people and their feelings. I feel more alive because I have more *empathy*. I do, and it's great.

Now that we have reviewed the pillars of DSD and have them front and center as we *dive* into the following chapters, where is the magic when it comes to using the methodology?

The magic lives right at the intersection of going *deep* and *staying shallow*. It is about gaining a fundamental understanding, not overthinking things; it's about touching base with what matters most while keeping things simple. This sweet spot is where life feels more focused and satisfying.

Going *deep* is essential. It lends *authenticity* to our understanding and enables us to break down complex, overwhelming topics into manageable pieces. This depth instills a sense of confidence within us.

On the flip side, there's a unique strength in *staying shallow*. It serves as a break from the relentless pace of daily life. It involves stripping away the non-essential, honing in on what brings us joy and tranquility. It also enables us to take our time with things. That's huge.

What are the genuinely confusing or complicated things in your life right now?

What are the things you dread doing?

What are the things you keep putting off?

Then, would understanding them better and simplifying them make you NOT dread doing them and STOP putting them off?

If not, you must cut them out of your life if possible.

If yes, the DSD methodology anchored in our pillars can help.

This dance, between depth and simplicity, can become a lifestyle. It's choosing to care more about the depth of your adventures and connections than how much you pack into your day—living in tune with what's truly important and finding your happy place in the simple things.

But you also have to be ready to *call a Spade a Spade*. We will take on this task together, with the pillars of DSD as our guides. We will *dive deep*, keep it real, and discover the joy of living a genuinely authentic life.

Let's revisit *Personal Growth* from Chapter 3 for a minute. In the quest for personal growth and self-improvement, individuals often struggle to balance *deep* exploration with simplicity. This delicate dance can lead to profound transformation and fulfillment.

In the rest of this chapter, we will add another element and explore the transformative power of vulnerability.

We will discuss practical ways to cultivate this quality in our lives and how the fusion of depth and simplicity and being vulnerable can lead to a more meaningful and gratifying life.

Self-awareness and vulnerability are the cornerstones of personal growth. They provide the foundation for building a more authentic and fulfilling life.

Self-awareness is the starting point, as it includes recognizing our strengths, weaknesses, emotions, thoughts, beliefs, and behaviors. Through *self-awareness*, we can identify areas that need improvement or change.

Vulnerability, on the other hand, is the path to *authenticity*. It means opening up about our fears, challenges, and weaknesses.

It requires courage and a willingness to expose our true selves despite the risks of judgment or rejection. Through vulnerability, we can foster *deeper* connections with others and live a life that is true to ourselves.

Some practical strategies can help us cultivate vulnerability in our lives.

Mindfulness practices, such as meditation or breathing exercises, can help us become more aware of our thoughts, feelings, and bodily sensations in the present moment.

I'm not going to lie. I have yet to embrace those. But even taking a moment to pause and take a beat is a good start.

After a nice run, I take the time to look around me, look at the sky, take a few *deep* breaths, and enjoy the moment.

Try that after your next run or walk.

As I mentioned, journaling can also be a powerful tool for self-reflection. It allows us to explore our experiences, emotions, and reactions to various situations and record them in writing.

Also, seeking feedback from trusted individuals can provide valuable insights into aspects of ourselves that we may need to be made aware of.

Working with a therapist or counselor can facilitate greater vulnerability and understanding. If needed, allow yourself to do that. Seriously.

Lastly, I love the phrase; *repetition is the mother of all learning.*

So, here is a quick recap. This fusion of depth and simplicity is where the magic happens. It is about diving *deep* into what truly matters while maintaining a simple, straightforward approach to life.

This fusion brings balance, focus, and clarity to our lives, leading to a more meaningful and fulfilling existence.

When we embrace depth, we enhance our understanding of the world and our place in it. We foster *deeper* connections with others and develop a profound appreciation for life's experiences.

Depth allows us to pursue meaningful goals and achievements, leading to personal satisfaction and fulfillment. It equips us with the emotional and intellectual tools to face challenges and builds *resilience*.

On the other hand, simplicity brings focus and clarity. It helps us remove unnecessary clutter, both physical and mental, allowing us to concentrate on what truly matters.

The fusion of depth and simplicity is a holistic approach to life. It prioritizes the quality of experiences and relationships over the quantity. It encourages us to live in a way that is true to our values and aspirations. It brings us inner peace and satisfaction as we find joy and importance in the right places.

Diving in leads to personal growth, a journey that requires effort and dedication. Personal growth helps us cultivate our *self-awareness* and vulnerability as we lay the groundwork for this transformation to more *authenticity*.

So, let us embark on this voyage with open hearts and curious minds, exploring the depths of our emotions and simplifying our lives to find true fulfillment.

Chapter End DSD:

Well, that's the rest of this book. OK, Let's Go!

> The best investment that you can make is in *yourself.*

Chapter End Notes

Chapter 7:

DSD.
into Politics.

Stay curious.
Never stop asking questions.

BE AUTHENTIC WITH YOURSELF.

Chapter 7: DSD into Politics

I know. I know. Trust me, I know.

I know this is a topic most people do not enjoy discussing, but stick with me, and I promise it won't be painful. I wanted to quickly cover it because politics led to all of this—all of it. But again, don't worry. This will be painless and not controversial but rather informative and enlightening.

Chapters 1-6 set the stage for everything we will now discuss. I wanted to ensure you understood how I shifted my mindset to the DSD methodology rooted in the four pillars to make sense of the world around me, starting in March 2020. That's why we have this chapter. The shift I experienced was because of politics.

That shift then started to permeate other areas of my life, sometimes without realizing it. I started *calling a Spade a Spade* with many things, starting with politics but continuing to my family life, relationships, social issues, health and wellness, and the most difficult one: myself.

Initially, I said this book is not about the coronavirus outbreak or politics.

It's not.

But I would be negligent and also not honest if I did not admit this. The politics that started in March

2020 was the impetus for my awakening and a newborn desire to engage with the news differently and more inquisitively.

It was politics that, for the first time in my life, actually affected my life and my daily freedom. It was politics that led to *Deep Shallow Dive* and gave birth to embracing *Calling a Spade a Spade*. Therefore, I would be remiss if I did not talk about it, so I owe it one quick and easy breezy chapter. Ok, let's get this over with.

Politics in the United States changed in 2016. Again, to be exact, it changed on Tuesday, November 8, 2016, around 11:30 pm PST/2:30 am EST. In one of the most shocking U.S. elections in modern political history, Donald J. Trump defeated Hillary Clinton.

Politics would change. The News Media would change. The Country would change. The Mood would change.

But I didn't! I did not change. Did you?

I will not harp on that much, but I do not think Trump was *supposed* to win. He just wasn't. It was a shock. His victory was a massive shock to everyone who was politically minded and considered to have insight.

Politics and political discourse would never be the same after this; the proof has been in the pudding.

We can all agree it has been different. To avoid getting bogged down in either President Trump's term or President Biden's, let's just group the years between 2016 and 2024 as a collective and acknowledge that politics, as a whole, have become different. As a country, we became political.

Agreed?

What started happening was that uncomfortable truths entered the fray. Politics took on a new realm where some uncomfortable truths that often lurked beneath the surface, never being acknowledged and addressed, started coming up for air.

But even when things came out, many wanted to avoid them. Especially those that it came out against. However, avoiding these uncomfortable truths can perpetuate corruption and inequality, leading to many negative consequences.

When uncomfortable truths are swept under the rug, the political process becomes less transparent, and hidden agendas and actions go unchecked. This lack of transparency can foster corruption, as those in power can maintain their authority without being held accountable for their actions.

Again, I am talking collectively and in general. This is not just about the White House but also our Congress, our state governments, and even our local governments.

This is why people cringe and shy away from discussing politics or even the word. Think about it. Are you like that? I used to be like that.

Moreover, the long-standing political avoidance of uncomfortable truths can result in policies and decisions that perpetuate or exacerbate inequality, discrimination, and social injustices. By brushing aside these uncomfortable truths, politicians fail to address the real issues facing marginalized communities, reinforcing existing disparities in areas such as education, healthcare, and economic opportunities. This not only hinders progress but also undermines the principles of democracy by limiting the free exchange of ideas and suppressing dissent.

So, how do we fix this? If I knew that solution, this book would sell a gazillion copies!

But I will say, a great place to start is by *calling a Spade a Spade* and trying to adhere to the approach of taking a *Deep Shallow Dive*, situation by situation, and evaluating each and everything in a silo.

This will be the most challenging concept to grasp because it will require those who lean to the right politically to slide more center and those who currently lean to the left politically to do the same. Now look to your right or left and say hello to your new friend. I promise we are all not that different.

Ok, in all seriousness, what do I mean by all that?

If we can all agree that the sheer nature of politics changed in 2016, then we must acknowledge that the politicians changed with it. The division and polarization that started and has continued are unlike anything our generation has seen.

The Baby Boomer generation, those born between 1946 and 1964, had some division and polarization due to the Cold War with the Soviet Union and various other tensions, such as in Vietnam.

For Generation X, those born between 1965 and 1980, politics has been relatively smooth sailing for the most part, besides some flair-ups in the Middle East and a few other parts of the world. But those events were things we watched on the nightly news and then moved on with our lives.

Yes, things have happened and taken place politically during the past forty years, but again, nothing caused the division that Trump's unexpected victory in 2016 or the coronavirus outbreak in 2020 caused. Do you agree?

Take one second now to think about your relationship with politics before 2016. Did you even have one? I did not.

However, as soon as Trump won the election, it brought on four years of nationwide division and mean Tweets. Then, 2020, with the coronavirus outbreak and all the controversy there, followed by the 2020 Election and all the subsequent turbulence and arguments that ensued.

Again, those occurrences collectively caused a change in our relationship with politics. That change started for some in 2016 after that election, others in 2020, and maybe never for some. I know a few people like that; lucky them, right!

But for the record, I am glad it happened to me, starting in March 2020. I feel more alive and aware because of it, and I am writing this book because of it.

Why am I glad that it happened to me?

As I said, politics is different now. It is a much more significant part of our daily lives and much more in our faces. Social Media has brought to light uncomfortable truths that have eroded public trust in government institutions and the political process. This has further exacerbated political divisions and hindered progress on important issues.

Also, as I stated earlier, avoiding uncomfortable truths can undermine the accountability of political leaders and institutions, making it challenging to hold them responsible for their failures and wrongdoings. This stifles progress on critical issues, which can lead to severe consequences for society.

These combined have adverse effects not only on our society but also on our spirit and well-being.

They can also negatively affect our relationships because of the strife and discord they cause.

They can even negatively affect our health and wellness; that is where I draw the line. I want to do everything I can to help prevent that from happening to you. Your health is important to me. It honestly is.

So, how do we counteract these adverse effects?

We *call a Spade a Spade* on everyone at all times, whenever it's warranted. This comes into play most with the people we like and support because that's when *calling a Spade a Spade* is uncomfortable and difficult.

But whether you voted for them or continue to support them, they are not doing everything right. It's just impossible. Think about it.

Do the people you love the most always do everything right? Does your spouse, kids, parents, boss, co-worker, teammate, or siblings?

Do YOU do everything right all the time?

I know I don't, and I am sure your answer is no. How can it be yes for our politicians? Think about that.

So, regarding our politicians and politics, embracing uncomfortable truths openly and honestly is crucial. Informed citizenship and political engagement have transformative potential in this regard. When citizens are well-informed about political issues and actively engage in the political process, we can advocate for policies that align with our values and address critical issues.

Our engagement also holds elected officials accountable for their actions and decisions, as politicians are more likely to respond to the needs of their constituents when they know they are being watched and evaluated.

Remember. They are people as well, just like you and me. They are parents, neighbors, friends, family members, husbands, wives, brothers, sisters, sons, and daughters. Again, just like you and me.

As informed citizens, we can voice our concerns, participate in civic activities, and vote. This empowerment fosters a sense of agency and ownership over the democratic process. It also drives social change by raising awareness about important issues, organizing protests, and advocating for justice and equality.

Political engagement often involves collaboration and community building, bringing people from *dive*rse backgrounds together to work toward shared goals and promote social cohesion. Finding information and educating yourself about political issues can lead to personal growth and a *deeper* understanding of complex topics. You will start to get it. Once you get it, it's up to you to do anything with it or have the peace of mind that you got it. Both are fine.

The power of embracing uncomfortable truths can lead to accountability and change in politics. Let me give you some examples. The #MeToo movement, for example, highlighted uncomfortable truths about sexual harassment and misconduct within the political and entertainment industries. As survivors shared their stories, it led to greater accountability for individuals accused of wrongdoing, resignations, and a broader cultural shift toward addressing these issues.

Another example is whistleblowers in government and corporations that often expose uncomfortable truths about wrongdoing, corruption, or abuse of power. Their actions can trigger investigations, legal actions, and calls for accountability.

Historical movements such as the Civil Rights Movement and Indigenous Rights movements confronted uncomfortable truths about racial discrimination, segregation, historical injustices, and cultural erasure. Through protests, advocacy, and public awareness campaigns, these movements brought about legal reforms, desegregation, indigenous rights recognition, and reconciliation efforts.

Climate change activism, social media activism, and protests against economic inequality have also forced governments and corporations to address uncomfortable truths and take action on pressing issues.

In all these examples, embracing uncomfortable truths was crucial in bringing about accountability and change in the political sphere. These revelations often sparked public outrage, legal actions, and movements to address systemic issues and drive positive transformation in society and politics.

Embracing uncomfortable political truths is essential for promoting transparency, accountability, and positive change. Avoiding these uncomfortable truths perpetuates corruption and inequality, diminishes public trust in political institutions, and hinders progress on critical issues.

However, through informed citizenship and political engagement, individuals can influence policy, hold elected officials accountable, drive social change, and promote community building. By acknowledging and addressing uncomfortable truths, we can create a more just and equitable political landscape that works for the betterment of all.

A very notable example of a political situation that was transformed through the embracing of uncomfortable truths is the exposure and subsequent fall of the apartheid regime in South Africa.

Apartheid was a system of institutionalized racial segregation and discrimination in South Africa that lasted from 1948 until the early 1990s. This regime enforced a harsh system of racial classification and segregation, denying fundamental rights to the majority non-white population of South Africa.

The realities of apartheid - systematic oppression, racial discrimination, and human rights abuses - were long ignored or rationalized by many, both within South Africa and in the international community. However, the relentless efforts of anti-apartheid activists brought these uncomfortable truths to the forefront of global awareness.

Key figures like Nelson Mandela, along with numerous activists within South Africa, played pivotal roles in exposing the brutal realities of apartheid. International movements, organizations, and influential personalities also contributed by imposing economic sanctions and cultural boycotts against South Africa.

The turning point came with increasing internal resistance and international pressure, leading to negotiations between the apartheid regime and the African National Congress. The establishment of the Truth and Reconciliation Commission (TRC) after the end of apartheid was a critical step in addressing the uncomfortable truths of the past.

The TRC, led by Archbishop Desmond Tutu, aimed to help heal the country by uncovering the truth about human rights violations during apartheid. The widespread acknowledgment of these uncomfortable truths, both domestically and internationally, was instrumental in dismantling the apartheid system.

In 1994, South Africa held its first democratic elections, marking the official end of apartheid and the election of Nelson Mandela as the country's first Black president. The transformation of the political situation in South Africa demonstrates how acknowledging and confronting uncomfortable truths can lead to profound change.

It set an example of how a nation could transition from systemic oppression to a more democratic and equitable system through truth, reconciliation, and collective action. This case is a poignant reminder of the power of confronting harsh realities, no matter how uncomfortable, to pave the way for political transformation and social healing. It highlights the importance of collective responsibility, the courage to face brutal truths, and the potential for change, even in seemingly intractable situations.

It reminds us of the potential for political transformation and social healing when brutal truths are confronted. Ultimately, embracing uncomfortable truths in politics is a catalyst for accountability, systemic change, and a more just and equitable society.

Chapter End DSD:

I appreciate you suffering through an entire chapter on politics, so I will not make you go through the agony of a Chapter End DSD. Instead, scan this QR code to listen to some of the best episodes.

Most are under 25 minutes, so they're perfect for binging on a drive or while you're getting your steps in. Scan the QR Code and listen:

SCAN ME

//DSD EXCLUSIVE EPISODES

www.deepshallowdive.com

Available on All Platforms!

Chapter End Notes

Chapter 8:

**DSD.
into Personal Relationships.**

Stay enthusiastic. Never stop engaging with others.

Chapter 8: DSD into Personal Relationships.

Okay, let's now discuss personal relationships, a topic hopefully less divisive and controversial than politics—although maybe not right! Like politics, there is a delicate balance between truth and discomfort in personal relationships. Let's *dive* into this chapter, as it will give you immediate tools and mindsets to apply to your life.

When it comes to personal relationships, many of us shy away from confronting uncomfortable truths, fearing the potential conflicts that might arise. We also avoid *Calling a Spade a Spade*, especially with those closest to us.

But what are the repercussions of avoiding these truths?

How can we harness the power of honest communication, *empathy*, and vulnerability to deepen our connections with others?

What would the benefits be if we did?

Would they outweigh the awkwardness?

Would our relationships become more authentic if we always said what is on our minds?

Would they then become better, stronger, and more fulfilling?

Let's see.

To begin with, let's discuss something we truly improve at with maturity, personal growth, and life experiences, and that is honest communication.

I am talking brutally honest, unfiltered communication—tough love, as they say. Honesty that even sometimes hurts. Honest communication is the cornerstone of any meaningful relationship. It builds trust, fosters understanding, resolves conflicts, and promotes *authenticity*.

When we communicate truthfully, we demonstrate our trustworthiness and sincerity, laying the foundation for a solid and lasting bond with one another—the type of bond that lasts forever and is unbreakable.

By openly addressing issues and finding solutions, we prevent resentments from festering and instead create an environment of genuine connection. This may seem obvious, and you may think you already do all that.

But do you? All the time? With everyone? I don't yet. But I am trying.

It's easy to address things when you agree with each other on something. But I am talking about addressing things when you disagree with what your loved one or friend says but do not want to make it contentious. Confronting those moments leads to actual growth in our relationships.

Nevertheless, those are also tricky conversations.

We all need help gaining perspective and navigating these difficult conversations. Sometimes, we also need the courage to initiate them. This is where *Calling a Spade a Spade* comes in handy.

When a relationship can handle honest communication, it is at its best. However, we must build up to that level of trust and openness.

One way to build to that is by embracing the DSD pillar of *empathy*. The ability to understand and share the emotions of others is a vital component of honest communication and leads to *deeper* connections.

When we empathize with people, we create a stronger emotional bond by validating their feelings. It enhances communication, supports vulnerability, and strengthens conflict resolution. We reduce misunderstandings and promote effective dialogue by genuinely listening and seeking to understand. Again, we must build to all this, especially with those closest to us.

Because, again, those closest to us are the ones we have the most difficulty talking our uncomfortable truths with. This is now even more complicated because our relationships are divided into two buckets and occur in two places:

Those buckets/places are real-life and online. Let's start by talking about our online relationships. It's disheartening to see the amount of intense and hostile arguments online these days. Over the past few years, online toxicity has become increasingly prominent, and you can again trace it back to 2020 and even 2016. This has caused a lot of tension for people and even within their families and friend groups.

What is the root cause of this? Well, I can tell you the root enabler. It's social media. Again, social media has provided the platform and, quite frankly, an invitation for this, as people engage online in ways they would never do face-to-face.

If you remember that far back, think about your online experience on social media before 2020, 2016, and then 2009.

I will refresh your memory for those active on social media from the beginning. For those that have not been, this will still be interesting.

Before 2009, it was Myspace. Tom from Myspace. Tom was everybody's friend. Before that, there was Friendster, but let's not worry about that. So, Myspace was most people's introduction to building personal relationships online.

Maybe it was the novelty of online social media or the lack of awareness of the controversial things taking place in the world, but Myspace was nice. It was fun. It was harmless for the most part until scams and porn infiltrated it. Even then, it was harmless to our relationships unless your significant other caught you doing something you should not have been doing. Yikes.

But it wasn't political. It wasn't argumentative. It wasn't toxic. It was just voyeuristic to an extent and maybe a time suck, but it was not nasty.

In 2009, Facebook surpassed Myspace as the most-visited social media website. Along with Twitter, they ushered in a new era of social media. Then, as the years progressed and they became more of a daily part of people's lives, they started to have the ability to affect our relationships. Social media began to take over or at least become a regular part of our daily lives.

There is a fascinating DSD that I will tackle on the podcast at some point. It explores how social media and its adoption from 2009 to 2016 could have led to Trump's remarkable victory in the 2016 election and, from 2016 to 2020, enabled an unprecedented level of division among people in the United States and even globally.

Social media, though, had become a force to be reckoned with and was here to stay. It had entered the chat, changing how we consumed news and opinions.

Now, imagine if there were no Facebook, Twitter, or YouTube. Would Trump have still won in 2016? And then again, without Facebook, Twitter, and YouTube from 2016 – 2020, would public discourse have been the same, and would the arguments and the fights and the hate have been able to flourish the way that it did?

Those sites provided the platform for that, so would the same level of division, arguments, fights, and hate exist if they did not exist? I don't think so because we would be unable to see it as we did on our computers and phones.

That is a *Deep Shallow Dive,* for sure.

Even though social media occurs online, it has been a pivotal part of our offline relationships, especially since 2020, when the coronavirus events played out. People started engaging in those platforms, seeking information but instead finding controversy.

On top of that, there is the 2020 election between Trump and Biden, and then there are various global news events. Ready? George Floyd, the January 6 Capital Riots, meme stock mania, the withdrawal of U.S. troops from Afghanistan, the Russia and Ukraine war, the Supreme Court overturning Roe v Wade, the Pro-democracy protests in Iran, Buffalo Bills safety Damar Hamlin cardiac episode on the football field, the Chinese spy balloon, the Titan submersible imploding and killing all five people on board, and the Hamas and Israel war. Wow.

Again, imagine seeing nothing about all those events on Facebook, Instagram, X, YouTube, and TikTok. Would the magnitude of the stories have been the same? Did the ability to see them on social media make them more significant?

Then, consider what else might have been happening while our attention was captivated by these events. Who knows, right?

Social media has not just been a backdrop; it has been the stage itself in the unfolding narrative of these events. Since 2020, our world has been inundated by captivating events. Each of these moments, be it the presidential showdown of Trump versus Biden, the outcry following George Floyd's death, or the heart-wrenching scenes from wars and protests, found a magnifying glass on platforms like Facebook, Instagram, X, and TikTok.

These social networks didn't just share news; they shaped the fabric of these stories' reach and resonance. Again, if we were to strip away social media's influence, would the impact of these events be felt as deeply?

This is the lens through which we must view our interconnected era—not just for the stories told but for the untold ones hidden by the shadows of trending hashtags and viral posts. That might be even more than a *Deep Shallow Dive*. That might be my next book concept!

What would life be like without social media?

How much more productive would we be?

Would there be less toxicity and vitriol hate in the world?

Those are fascinating questions.

For now, though, I want to discuss things we can practice and incorporate into our lives to help us use the DSD methodology and the pillars we have discussed. This will help us understand and improve our relationships.

The hardest part about this is that it starts with YOU. Doing a *Deep Shallow Dive* into your relationships begins with doing *a Deep Shallow Dive* into YOU.

And that starts with you allowing yourself to be vulnerable. This is hard. I'm terrible at it.

But vulnerability, often seen as a sign of weakness, is a profound strength. We deepen emotional intimacy and connection when we open ourselves up and allow ourselves to be vulnerable. We reveal our true selves, including our fears, insecurities, and desires. This fosters trust, strengthens bonds, and encourages support.

By embracing vulnerability, we create a safe space and invite reciprocation from our loved ones. Being vulnerable is a rare character trait that touches on all four pillars of the DSD methodology:

Self-awareness: They almost go hand in hand. You indisputably get in touch with yourself.

Resilience: This is the byproduct. It makes you stronger. This happens.

Authenticity: The more vulnerable you are, the more *authentic* you become.

Empathy: You show your emotions, allowing others to foster *empathy* for you. That's okay, as mutual *empathy* strengthens your relationship bond. Our bonds are much more robust and rock-solid.

Okay, it's time to get real and raw again. Not allowing myself to be vulnerable is an uncomfortable truth for me.

I will admit it here in writing: It has kept me from certain things others have—important things—things that cause regrets. That's hard for me to admit, and it hurts, but it's the truth. I have never really allowed myself to embrace vulnerability as an asset until recently.

But I have tried to stop harping on the past and get better at this.

In my journey of self-discovery, personal growth, and relationship building, I have recognized vulnerability as a crucial trait and a cornerstone of *deep* and meaningful connections.

This silent strength is at the heart of the DSD methodology's four pillars, each representing a fundamental aspect of our human experience. Let's delve into the pillars more and consider how they can help foster an appreciation for vulnerability.

We will start with *self-awareness*. *Self-awareness*, that profound reflection inward, becomes truly attainable when we allow ourselves to be vulnerable. In this tender state, the pillar of *resilience* emerges, not despite our perceived weaknesses but because of them. It is a testament to our growth and a measure of the grit that vulnerability cultivates.

As we become more self-aware and resilient and then embrace the next pillar of *authenticity*, we find that vulnerability is the most genuine expression of *authenticity*. It takes a unique brand of courage to be truthful and stand naked in the face of judgment. Yet, this very act endears us to others, inviting a shared genuineness that can turn acquaintances into friends—real friends.

And then there's *empathy*, the most sacred of human connections. By being vulnerable, we not only become attuned to the nuances of our own emotions but also unlock the capacity to share in the emotions of others genuinely. This reciprocity of understanding and feeling forges bonds of a rare blend—resilient yet flexible, firm yet understanding.

For so long, I held vulnerability at arm's length, a self-imposed exile from the essence that makes relationships flourish. Admitting this uncomfortable truth has been a watershed moment for me, relinquishing old defenses. It's a declaration that I am ready to let down those walls, to let in the light of genuine connection.

Embracing vulnerability is perhaps the most potent act of self-love and love for others—it's an embrace I now welcome with open arms, ready for the mutual benefits and deepened bonds it promises.

I'm glad I got that off my chest. That was #realtalk. Thank you. This is the only way.

Okay. Moving on.

Now that we understand the importance of vulnerability, let's discuss uncomfortable truths in our relationships. While undeniably challenging, confronting uncomfortable truths in relationships is a necessary step toward cultivating healthy, authentic, and fulfilling ones.

It requires courage, effective communication skills, and a steadfast commitment to the relationship's well-being. Honest communication, compassion, and vulnerability are the columns upon which the confrontation of uncomfortable truths stands.

The easiest way to uncover our relationships' uncomfortable truths is again to *call a Spade a Spade*. But that is hard. Unlike politics, where there is usually no personal connection with the candidates or politicians, our relationships are rooted in that.

The truth is, it is hard to *call a Spade a Spade* on the people closest to you all the time. I get that. I know it is hard to *call a Spade a Spade* on your husband, wife, parents, brother, sister, boss, co-worker, or even your kids, but we have to try.

Let's build some skill sets to help us move towards this so that we are better equipped to think through the situations between us and our loved ones. Let's focus on building these skill sets and having the right mentality.

Just as our DSD pillars start with *self-awareness*, allow us to begin with the skill set of self-reflection. **Self-reflection** is the first step on this path. Take the time to be introspective and identify the uncomfortable truths within yourself. Ask probing questions and be honest about your feelings, beliefs, and behaviors affecting your relationships.

I have tried to get better at this.

What is bothering me?

What should I discuss with my loved ones or those I care about?

That answer typically solves the problem if I am willing to be vulnerable and authentic enough to express it clearly. But that is hard sometimes, depending on what it is.

However, building self-reflection into your mindset and skill set will allow you to have a more authentic relationship with yourself. Simply admitting there is something, even if only to yourself, is that forward momentum we discussed. It will help you better navigate the path toward personal growth and *deeper* connections. Remember, we always want forward momentum.

We also always want those small wins.

The following skill set to try and build is **initiating open and honest conversations**—not during a fight or argument but when you are calm and not in the heat of the moment. This seems obvious, but bringing something up during these quiet times is hard. They say timing is everything in relationships, and this is called proactive timing.

If you can do this and express your thoughts, feelings, and concerns calmly and clearly, it encourages them to do the same. One way to help with this is to pause and listen. Active listening is crucial during these conversations. Give your full attention, show compassion, and avoid interrupting or jumping to conclusions.

This creates a space for understanding and *empathy* to flourish by genuinely hearing each other. Ensure both sides are in the mood to talk, not distracted by their phones, and not in a rush.

Honestly, initiating open and honest conversations might be easier for women than for men. I don't know many good guys at this—I know I'm not! That's just more #realtalk right there.

The next skill set is also one of our DSD pillars, and if you can't tell yet, it is one of my favorite things to discuss: **empathy**. Developing empathy comes naturally to some, or it can be a skill that can be honed over time for others.

To hone this, work on understanding the perspectives and emotions of others by putting yourself in their shoes. Acknowledge their feelings and validate their experiences. This kindhearted approach fosters *deeper* connections and creates a more compassionate and harmonious relationship.

Next, **seeking feedback** is an often overlooked skill set and activity that only some of us are in the habit of doing. Seek input from your loved ones about your behavior, communication style, and how you can improve the relationship.

Be open to constructive criticism and use it as an opportunity for growth. Apologize sincerely when you make mistakes or hurt someone, and be willing to forgive others when they apologize. Forgiveness is a powerful tool for healing and moving forward.

To also help navigate uncomfortable truths in relationships, using "I" statements, such as "I feel" or "I think," allows individuals to express their perspectives without placing blame. Being specific about the issue and articulating why it is the concern prevents vagueness and misunderstandings.

In summary, confronting uncomfortable truths is a necessary and transformative process in personal relationships. So, embrace the discomfort, for it is through these uncomfortable truths that we uncover the depths of ourselves and forge *deeper* connections with others.

Chapter End DSD:

GO DEEP:

We are back at it; I hope you enjoyed your two chapters off from this! But let's revisit our DSD Chapter End methodology for personal relationships now. Please think about someone you want to have a better relationship with. This can be a family member, friend, boss, co-worker, or even an ex! Mad props to you if you picked that one.

But I want this person to be someone important to you and someone you want to have a better relationship with.

Write their name here:

Using the DSD methodology, let's tackle the example of improving a relationship with a close family member, perhaps a sibling. I am blessed to have a wonderful relationship with my brother. But coming out of COVID-19 and the past two Presidential Elections, I know far too many siblings whose relationships have been strained or broken because of differences in opinions about COVID-19 protocols or political beliefs.

I hope this is not you, but if so, I hope this outline helps.

Imagine you and your sibling have grown apart due to unspoken grievances. To go *deep* and initiate a conversation aimed at improving the relationship with your sibling, here's a step-by-step gameplan:

Step 1: Self-Reflection:

Before initiating the conversation, spend some time reflecting on the relationship. Consider what has led to the current state of distance or conflict. Understand your feelings, identify the issues you want to address, and clarify your goals for the conversation.

Please write it down this time on paper, not on your phone. There are some extra pages in the back for this if you like. You will take this with you when you have this talk. It shows respect for repairing your relationship because you took the time to write it down.

Step 2: Prepare:

Think about what you want to say. Write down key points to ensure you cover everything necessary without getting sidetracked. Decide on the best time and place for the conversation—a setting where you both feel comfortable and won't be interrupted.

Step 3: Invitation to Talk:

Reach out to your sibling. You might say, "I've been thinking about us and how we've grown apart. Could we set aside some time to talk? I value our relationship and would also like to understand your feelings."

Step 4: Set the Tone:

As you begin the conversation, make it clear that you intend to understand and improve your relationship, not to criticize or argue. You could start with, "I want to talk about how we can grow closer again because our relationship means a lot to me."

Step 5: Active Listening:

After sharing your thoughts, give your sibling the space to respond. Practice active listening: maintain eye contact, nod to show you're following, and don't interrupt. I repeat, do not interrupt.

Validate their feelings by saying, "I understand why you'd feel that way." If this conversation is not in person but over the phone, pause and refrain from interrupting while they are talking or responding.

Step 6: Share and Empathize:

When it's your turn to speak, use "I" statements to express your feelings without placing blame, such as, "I feel sad that we don't spend much time together." Show *empathy* by trying to see the situation from their perspective.

Step 7: Seek Common Ground:

Look for common ground or shared experiences that can serve as a foundation for rebuilding your relationship. It could be positive childhood memories or shared interests.

Step 8: Actionable Steps:

Decide on actionable steps you can both take to improve the relationship. These include regular check-ins, shared activities, or simply a commitment to communicate more honestly.

Step 9: Follow-Up:

After the conversation, take time to reflect on what was said. Please send a message to your sibling thanking them for the talk and reiterating your commitment to the action steps you've agreed upon.

Remember, going *deep* is not a one-time event but the beginning of an ongoing process of building a stronger, more honest relationship with your sibling. It requires patience, understanding, and consistent effort from both parties.

STAY SHALLOW:

Going *deep* per above will be hard—I get that—but it will also be worth it. This relationship we are rebuilding matters to you, and like everything in life that matters, it takes time and care to nurture it back.

However, one thing that will help, especially in personal relationships, is to keep things straightforward. This is where staying *shallow* will help.

Staying *shallow* in improving a sibling relationship involves taking small, manageable steps that are not always about *deep* emotional discussions but foster a sense of connection and goodwill.

Here's how you can do it:

Step 1: Start Light:

Start with light and easy topics. Discuss common interests you have previously had, share some funny recent stories if you have any, or talk about neutral subjects like your spouses, kids, movies, books, sports, TV shows, or any shared hobbies.

For now, avoid bringing up past conflicts or *deep* emotional issues. Reconnect a bit and get the conversation flowing. Ideally, have a few laughs, but more importantly, break the ice with each other.

Step 2: Regular Check-Ins:

At the end of the conversation, commit to checking in regularly. This could be a simple text message, a quick phone call, or a comment on their social media post. The idea is to maintain contact without delving into anything too serious.

Step 3: Share Positive News:

When you have good news or something positive happens in your life, share it with your sibling. Texting is fine. However, nothing takes the place of the old-fashioned phone call.

Call if you can, but texting is better than nothing.

Step 4: Engage in Shared Activities:

If your proximity allows for this, plan activities you both enjoy. Walking, hiking, engaging in a shared hobby, or grabbing lunch. Shared experiences can strengthen your bond without the need for *deep* conversations.

You can do this collectively as a family, but make time for that one-on-one time with your sibling. Even if that is just a phone call, commit to doing it.

Step 5: Celebrate Special Occasions:

Remember and acknowledge special occasions like birthdays, anniversaries, or significant achievements. Again, pick up the phone and call. These special occasions deserve more than a text message.

Step 6: Offer Help When Needed:

If your sibling is going through a tough time or needs assistance, offer help in practical ways. This could be running errands, helping with a project, or being there to listen if they want to talk.

This is something that ideally propels the relationship back to better times, but even if not, it is the right thing to do.

Step 7: Use Humor:

A shared laugh can be a powerful tool in healing and improving relationships. Use humor to keep interactions enjoyable and to break any tension. Whether this is sending them a viral video clip, a funny meme, or a GIF, laughter truly is one of the best medicines for rebuilding relationships.

When you can laugh together, the defenses come down, and that happiness allows for a more genuine connection to return.

Step 8: Respect Boundaries:

Rome and this book were not built and written in a day, and rebuilding a personal relationship will likely not either. Understand and respect each other's boundaries. If your sibling isn't ready for *deeper* engagement, don't push it. Respect their space and continue with your light but positive interactions.

Step 9: Be Consistent:

Consistency is always key. Regular, positive interactions, even if not super *deep*, can gradually improve the overall quality of your relationship. Make it a priority. Make them a priority.

Step 10: Be Patient:

This will be one of the most challenging things for many of you. Understand that repairing and improving a relationship takes time. Take your time with the process. Allow the relationship to grow at a comfortable pace for both of you.

By staying *shallow*, you nurture the relationship gently without the pressure to address *deeper* issues before both parties are ready. This approach can lay the groundwork for more meaningful interactions in the future.

DIVE IN:

Honestly, this is the most meaningful section for me. If this book, this chapter, and the DSD methodology can help repair one personal relationship that you have in your life, whether that is a sibling or someone else, then all the hard work and time it took to bring this book to fruition has been worth it. I mean that.

To *dive* in is about fully committing to rebuilding and enhancing your relationship with your sibling, integrating both the *Go Deep* and *Stay Shallow* strategies. I want you to *dive* in.

Here's a step-by-step approach:

Step 1: Act on Your Insights:

Start implementing the more profound understanding and insights gained from your *Go Deep* conversation.

Use this new knowledge actively in your interactions, showing that you've listened and are trying to change and improve the relationship.

Step 2: Regularly Engage in Meaningful Activities:

Plan and participate in activities you and your sibling enjoy, which you identified in the *Stay Shallow* phase. These could be shared hobbies, outings, or even simple activities like having a meal together.

The key is to make these interactions regular and meaningful.

Step 3: Keep Communication Open:

Continue communicating openly and honestly, as established in the *Go Deep* phase.

Encourage your sibling to share their thoughts and feelings, showing that you are there to listen and engage genuinely.

Step 4: Address Issues as They Arise:

This is huge. Instead of letting problems fester, address them as they come up. Use the communication skills you've developed to discuss issues calmly and empathetically.

Step 5: Show Gratitude and Acknowledgment:

Regularly express gratitude and appreciation for your sibling. Acknowledge their efforts to improve the relationship, and be vocal about the positive aspects you observe. Even if just via text, say it. Let them know.

Step 6: Celebrate Progress:

Acknowledge and celebrate the progress you both make in this relationship. This could be as simple as acknowledging how much you enjoyed spending time together or how a recent conversation brought you closer. Again, say it. Let them know what you are feeling.

Step 7: Continue Self-Reflection and Growth:

Keep reflecting on your behavior and growth. Stay open to feedback from your sibling and be willing to continue working on yourself to improve the relationship. This will also help you hone in on that DSD pillar of *self-awareness* with yourself.

Step 8: Consistency and Patience:

Be consistent in your efforts and patient with the process. Again, rebuilding a solid relationship takes time, and showing that you are committed to this over the long term is crucial.

In summary, use your shared history as a foundation to build new, positive memories. Sharing old photos, reminiscing about childhood memories, or creating new experiences can strengthen your bond.

If this exercise was about your sibling, remember that siblings are something you don't get more of, like parents. They are family, and family truly is what matters the most.

By *Diving In*, you are actively working on mending the more profound aspects of your relationship with the daily, lighter interactions, leading to a more open, fulfilling, and genuine connection with your sibling.

Through this practical application of the DSD methodology, you can gradually transform your relationship with your sibling or others, moving from a place of distance to one of newfound closeness and restrengthened ties.

This chapter can help you repair a relationship with a loved one. Repairing a relationship with a loved one goes beyond mere reconciliation; it's about rebuilding trust, understanding, and compassion that may have been lost.

This chapter aims to provide you with the tools and insights necessary to navigate the complexities of mending relationships. It emphasizes the profound impact of a harmonious family dynamic on your emotional and psychological well-being.

Strengthening these bonds can lead to a more supportive and fulfilling life, underscoring the irreplaceable value of family connections on our road toward personal growth and happiness.

It's about seeing the big picture – how getting along better with those you care about isn't just nice. It's a game-changer for our happiness and growth.

By embracing these ideas, we're not just fixing the occasional spat; we're building a family vibe about backing each other up, growing together, and having a lot of fun.

Please let me know if it does, as that will bring me joy. This was my favorite chapter to write about, and it took me the longest.

Writing this chapter was also very cathartic for me.

Any feedback is more than just words to me; it's a heartfelt echo of the journey we've taken together through this chapter. You can reach me anyway below; I would love to hear from you on this or anything else:

Chapter End Notes

BE AUTHENTIC WITH YOURSELF.

Chapter 9:

DSD.
into Social Issues.

Stay empowered.
Never stop taking action for your beliefs.

@DEEPSHALLOWDIVE

Chapter 9: DSD into Social Issues.

The previous chapters about politics and relationships are two areas we are accustomed to collectively addressing as a society, but not this next topic.

Social issues are not new, but they have hit the mainstream and the zeitgeist over the past decade. This could be again due to social media and the ability to see these social issues so much easier on our phones.

Regardless, social problems are now front and center and here to stay.

In this chapter, we explore the significance of addressing uncomfortable truths about social and societal issues and how individuals can contribute to positive social change by confronting these truths.

We also discuss the challenges and obstacles individuals may face in this process. Like in politics and relationships, confronting uncomfortable truths about social issues is crucial in our steps toward personal growth and self-discovery.

Addressing uncomfortable truths about social and societal issues is also significant and necessary for positive social change.

It has emerged hand in hand with the growth of social media because, again, we see what is taking place in real-time now from real people sharing what they see and deem the truth.

It is through this confrontation that we can understand social justice. We can raise awareness. We can encourage accountability. We can drive positive change and hopefully prevent damaging escalation. This can help empower marginalized groups. It can help foster dialogue. It can catalyze social movements and improve policy. Most of all, it can enhance our collective *resilience*, promote human rights, and create a more inclusive society.

To illustrate the impact of confronting uncomfortable truths, at the end of this chapter, in place of the DSD Chapter End, we will examine the global response to the HIV/AIDS epidemic as a prime example of positive change resulting from acknowledging uncomfortable truths.

Remember, besides natural disasters, things don't just happen. Human beings make them happen, and therefore, we can change them. We do not get everything right on the first take, especially regarding societal issues. Addressing uncomfortable truths about societal matters is significant for several reasons.

First, addressing inherent inequalities and injustices promotes communal justice and equality.

By acknowledging these uncomfortable truths, society can work towards correcting systemic biases and advancing human rights. It also makes us feel more in touch with our communities.

Secondly, confronting uncomfortable truths regarding social issues fosters informed public discourse. It allows for a more comprehensive understanding of societal issues and leads to better-informed citizens and effective policymaking. It also makes everyone feel more engaged, involved, and aware.

Thirdly, it drives meaningful change by serving as the first step toward developing solutions and strategies to address these problems. Addressing uncomfortable truths about societal issues is significant and necessary for fundamental social change. Remember, through this confrontation, we can promote humanitarian justice, raise awareness, encourage accountability, and ideally prevent unneeded escalation. In a nutshell, we can do what's right.

During the 1950s and 1960s, society was forced to come to terms with the uncomfortable reality of racial segregation, discrimination, and inequality. This led to significant legislative changes, such as the Civil Rights Act of 1964 and the Voting Rights Act of 1965. This was an example of a *Deep Shallow Dive* pillar coming through. *Resilience* led the way by encouraging individuals to look beyond surface-level knowledge and explore the underlying causes of inequality.

The Women's Suffrage Movement significantly challenged the uncomfortable truth of women's lack of political rights. Eventually, it gave women the right to vote in many countries. By delving *deep* into the gender dynamics and historical contexts surrounding women's rights struggles across different cultures and periods, society gained a comprehensive understanding of gender inequality. This knowledge and *empathy* empowered individuals to advocate for gender equality in various spheres of life.

In our previous discussion, we talked about the Anti-Apartheid Movement, which bravely confronted the uncomfortable reality of racial segregation and discrimination in South Africa. This movement played a significant role in the eventual dismantling of apartheid. Through a thorough investigation of colonial history and the systemic racism deeply ingrained in institutions such as education or employment systems, *self-awareness,* and *resilience* helped people gain valuable insights into how these institutions perpetuated injustice even after legal changes were made. Armed with this knowledge, they worked toward dismantling that oppressive system.

The LGBTQ+ rights movements have also emerged from confronting uncomfortable truths about discrimination against sexual and gender minorities. Diving into the complexities of sexual orientation, gender identity, and societal norms can foster *empathy* and understanding, leading to greater acceptance and support for LGBTQ+ rights. At the end of the day, people are people, and we all only have one life. So let everyone live it the way they want, as long as it does not infringe on others.

Environmental movements confront the uncomfortable truths of climate change, deforestation, pollution, and resource depletion. Although controversial, by diving into scientific research and understanding the interconnectedness of ecosystems, individuals can recognize the urgency of addressing real environmental issues. This knowledge empowers individuals to take sustainable actions in their own lives while advocating for systemic changes.

Lastly, the Immigrant rights movements confront uncomfortable truths about xenophobia, discrimination, and policies that marginalize migrant communities. By examining historical migration patterns and economic factors driving immigration flows through the lens of *resilience* and *authenticity*, individuals can gain a nuanced understanding of the challenges immigrants face.

This awareness fosters *empathy* and motivates individuals to actively support immigrant rights initiatives as long as they are correctly done and per a legal protocol. This is not about illegal immigration but rather the legal immigration that truly is the backbone of the United States of America.

These complex topics could warrant an entire chapter or even a book. Nevertheless, for now, we wanted to share them as examples of social and societal issues involving topics with uncomfortable truths attached to them.

We have dedicated episodes on the podcast to provide you with a solid foundation of understanding and awareness of these as DSDs. At their core, these topics center around a group needing support from those who champion their cause.

The individual is vital in promoting positive social change by confronting uncomfortable truths. They often have a more personal stake in these issues than policymakers. It all begins with raising awareness, and thanks to social media and the ability to broadcast directly from one's phone, individuals now have an unprecedented platform to make their voices heard.

All of this, though, requires one thing: to *call a Spade a Spade*. To *call a Spade a Spade* does indeed come with a level of anxiety due to the ability for extreme or detrimental viewpoints to gain an audience. Still, the overall benefits that have come with the empowering of the individual are worth protecting this ability and freedom of expression.

On an individual level, confronting the world's uncomfortable truths about societal issues promotes awareness by challenging others to think critically and develop a *deeper* understanding of the world around them. It also inspires action and advocacy by raising awareness of the more challenging aspects of societal problems and galvanizing movements for change. It creates that forward momentum.

It all starts with learning and educating yourself. For starters, podcasts have emerged as an incredible way to learn about various topics from people who take the time to do the research and are willing to present that to you.

We try and do that on our podcast, so whether it's the *Deep Shallow Dive* or others, find a few podcasts you like so you can listen to them while you go for a walk or are on the treadmill, or listen to them during a drive.

You can also educate yourself by learning about societal issues' historical and current contexts. Both. Believe it or not, YouTube and TikTok are two great places that provide educational videos. Great books, the Internet, using new tools like ChatGPT, and leveraging AI for its ability to gather and present information quickly and effectively are also excellent sources of education. Remember again, with all these, another human being wrote, filmed, and created the content you are consuming.

Therefore, recall what Steve Jobs said and think critically for yourself.

When you pick a topic you want to understand better, I highly recommend immersing yourself in all these platforms rather than just watching one or two pieces of content on one. You want to try to see trends and determine consensus. Once you watch dozens of takes on the same subject, you will start to see those trends, and ideally, things will begin to make more sense and fall into place.

Again, remember, we all have inherent biases, and independent content creators, mainstream media, and media generally have personal biases. Reflecting on personal biases and beliefs is crucial for personal growth and contributes to holistic understanding. Then, *call a Spade a Spade*. It lets you be more honest about the topic and prepares you to have better conversations about it.

Once you learn how to do this properly, engaging in open conversations about uncomfortable truths on social issues with family, friends, and colleagues deepens your relationships. It scopes them up and gives them more substance. Leveraging the DSD methodology and using the pillars we have discussed helps remove the raw emotion from complex topics and provides that much-needed backdrop of facts and historical context.

Remember, confronting uncomfortable truths in everything, especially social issues, is challenging. When it comes to the DSD methodology, *resilience* is required. Trying to achieve any meaningful positive social change will face resistance, which can sometimes be significant depending on the complexity of the topic.

However, the small steps individuals take, when multiplied by the efforts of many, can lead to significant progress. By addressing uncomfortable truths, individuals can work towards creating a more just, equitable, and compassionate society where the needs and rights of all members are respected and upheld.

Instead of the Chapter End DSD, let's *dive* into the global response to the HIV/AIDS epidemic to exemplify the positive impact of confronting that significant, uncomfortable truth. In the early 1980s, HIV/AIDS emerged as a devastating health crisis. Initially misunderstood and stigmatized, it was often labeled as a gay disease. However, significant progress was made by acknowledging the uncomfortable truths surrounding the epidemic.

Activists, health professionals, and affected communities confronted the stigmas and demanded better research and treatment options. Public education campaigns were initiated to spread awareness and reduce stigma. Support networks were established to provide medical care and social support.

And then, in 1991, basketball superstar Earvin "Magic" Johnson shocked the world when he announced he was HIV-positive. That one person and his individual decision to demonstrate *self-awareness, resilience, authenticity*, and *empathy* allowed for the shame of contracting HIV to be removed for countless others and enabled forward momentum.

His announcement improved treatments and reduced stigma and discrimination, policy changes, and a sense of global awareness and solidarity. The response to the HIV/AIDS crisis serves as a testament to the power of confronting uncomfortable truths. It showcases how societal attitudes and policies can be transformed through advocacy, education, and the courage to address complex issues head-on.

In summary, we can all contribute to a more just, informed, and empathetic society by acknowledging social and societal issues and working toward their resolution.

Chapter End Notes

Chapter 10:

DSD.
into Family Life.

Stay determined.
Never stop striving to make things better.

@DEEPSHALLOWDIVE

Chapter 10: DSD into Family Life.

This chapter encompasses much of what we discussed in Chapter 8 and *Personal Relationships*. Still, I wanted to give it a dedicated chapter because family is at the core of my belief system and a value I cherish.

As the world becomes increasingly complicated, I wish for all of you to have your family or even friends that you consider family there to provide support, love, and companionship. Therefore, let's see if we can leverage the DSD methodology and our four pillars to strengthen this.

Since family life and personal relationships overlap, I will compose this chapter slightly differently. I will highlight topics that cause problems and then give solutions to help alleviate them. With any luck, you will come away with additional strategies and insights to improve your family life.

Remember, family is one thing we don't choose, and we only get one of them. I know they are not perfect—no one's family is—but when cared for, that family bond is irreplaceable.

Ok. Let's *dive* in. In the intricate family life network, unresolved problems, generational differences, and uncomfortable truths can lead to tension, emotional distress, and unnecessary drama. These uncomfortable truths may include communication breakdowns, past conflicts, differences in values and beliefs, parental favoritism, and financial issues.

They can include mental health problems, substance abuse, and divorce. Conflicts can arise when caring for aging parents, or if secrets and lies are exposed, and even sibling rivalry and jealousy. These issues can intertwine and create ongoing family drama, but addressing them is crucial for healing and improving family dynamics.

Once again, open and honest communication is the foundation for the healing and improving these family relationships.

Let's start by diving into why issues arise within families to get them on your radar. As you think about your family life and when problems come up, chances are they might fall into one of these categories:

Communication Breakdowns: The Silent Destroyer

One of the most prevalent issues within families is poor communication or a complete lack thereof. When family members struggle to express their feelings effectively, misunderstandings and unresolved conflicts arise, festering beneath the surface. Tension and resentment build, eroding the foundation of trust and understanding fundamental for a healthy family dynamic.

I have said it before and will repeat it: Open and honest communication and allowing yourself to be vulnerable are the gateways to *authenticity* and building *resilience*. They awaken your *self-awareness* and push you to embrace *empathy* in your mindset—all four DSD pillars.

Unresolved Past Traumas: The Ghosts of Christmas Past

Traumatic events from the past, such as abuse, neglect, or significant loss, can cast a long shadow on family dynamics. These unresolved traumas, buried *deep* within the family's collective consciousness, affect current relationships and behaviors. Unless these wounds are acknowledged and addressed, they continue to haunt the family, perpetuating cycles of pain and dysfunction.

Many people seek the assistance of a professional in this area, which is an excellent idea if you need help bringing this to the forefront. Find your path to resolving past traumas, as not all approaches work for everyone.

Generational Trauma: The Inherited Burden

Some family traumas can even be passed down through generations, leaving an indelible mark on the family. Whether through learned behaviors or as a consequence of historical events that have impacted the family, generational trauma can shape the way family members perceive themselves and others. Unraveling the threads of this inherited burden is essential for healing and breaking free from the chains of the past.

Parent-Child Role Reversal: The Burden of Care

In some families, as parents age, the lines between parent and child become blurred as children take on caregiving or emotional support roles for their parents. This role reversal can lead to resentment and conflict as the boundaries of responsibility become muddled. Navigating this delicate balance requires open communication and a mutual understanding of one another's needs and limitations. I want to expand on this one because I have personally had a lot of experience with this with my parents, and so hopefully, this can add value and help you think through your situation.

We all think of our parents as invincible, especially our fathers. I know I did. But there will come a time when this changes, and you realize that as they age and the world changes, you may have better skill sets to help them navigate life than they do, especially regarding their health.

This is what took place with my Dad in 2004 when he started to complain about chest pains while walking. This was the first time for me, now as an adult, to deal with a medical condition for him. I quickly realized that I was better suited and equipped than he was to research all of his symptoms and try to create the proper course of action.

My Dad was a true intellect, having been a college professor and a problem solver his entire life. But then, at 74, and in an online world, I asked him if I could take the lead in managing this situation. That was the first step to fostering this new role. I enrolled him in that decision.

Now, I was incredibly fortunate to have a father who was forward-thinking enough and also one who allowed his children to help. However, I still enrolled him in the process of letting me take the lead, and then I would explain to him the various things I was researching and why we should take the course of action that I would advocate.

The first step was to visit several cardiologists to get multiple opinions. I greatly respect the medical profession and those who sacrifice to become doctors or nurses. However, like any other industry, medicine is also a business.

When diagnosing a non-straightforward condition, such as heart-related issues, it is essential to consider all possible courses of action. It's not like healing a broken arm with limited treatment options.

Regarding my father's health condition, it was discovered that he had some blockages. After gathering opinions from some of the top cardiologists in California and the internationally renowned Cleveland Clinic, we embarked on a non-surgical intervention plan centered around losing weight and monitoring for any symptoms that could be warning signs. We determined that undergoing open-heart surgery would not enhance his quality of life and, as a result, the potential risks associated with the surgery outweighed any possible benefits.

The entire process brought my relationship with my Dad closer and enabled a shift from father/son to friends, good friends. Whether it was the fifteen minutes in the waiting rooms before appointments, the drive to the appointments, or even sharing the data and research I found with him, it transformed our relationship into something far more meaningful to me.

Before he passed, the remaining eleven years of my Dad's life continued along this new path. It gave me so much joy and fulfillment to know that I could do something for him and pay him back for all the fantastic things he did for me. I viewed that as an immense privilege and pleasure.

I know all parents are different; again, they must be open to accepting help and allowing themselves to be vulnerable, especially to their children. Regardless, I encourage you to embrace the opportunity or occurrences where your parents need help managing their health or any other aspect and see how you can support them.

If it ever happens, I hope it works out for you as it did for me. We can then change the name of this part from 'The Burden of Care' to 'The Blessing of Caring.' Being able to assist him was indeed a blessing to me.

Differing Values and Beliefs: The Clash of Generations

As younger generations grow and develop their values and beliefs, clashes with the older generations' traditions and perspectives are inevitable. These generational conflicts can divide the family as each side struggles to reconcile its deeply ingrained beliefs with the ever-changing world. Bridging this gap requires *empathy*, open-mindedness, and a willingness to find common ground.

Over the past few years, political debates have boiled over and spilled into family discussions. Again, many of these have centered around the divisiveness of Trump's win in 2016 and the varying opinions on the coronavirus pandemic. Both have fueled the fire.

In addition, international issues like the conflict in Gaza and hot topics like the potential TikTok ban have all been on the family debate menu. These events have highlighted the cultural and generational divides we're navigating.

Generational divides often arise from the unique social, technological, and political landscapes that different age groups grow up with or adapt to over time. They can manifest across a variety of specific topics.

Here are some examples:

1. Social Media and Online Privacy:

Older generations may prioritize privacy and be more skeptical of sharing personal information online. In comparison, younger generations are often more comfortable with social media platforms and publicly sharing aspects of their lives.

2. Same-Sex Marriage and LGBTQ+ Rights:

Older generations have witnessed significant shifts in the social acceptance of LGBTQ+ individuals and their rights, including marriage equality. Younger generations are more likely to take these rights as a given and may be more accepting of a spectrum of sexual orientations and gender identities.

3. Cannabis Legalization:

Attitudes towards the legalization of cannabis can vary, with younger generations often more in favor of legalization for medicinal and recreational use.

At the same time, older individuals may hold reservations due to the historical stigma.

4. Immigration:

Different generations can have varying perspectives on immigration, influenced by historical contexts, economic conditions, and cultural attitudes prevalent during their formative years.

This has also become highly partisan and political.

5. Education Reform:

There may be generational divides on the purpose of education, the importance of standardized testing, college affordability, and student loan debt, with younger individuals feeling the current pressures more acutely.

This has also become highly partisan and political.

6. Healthcare:

Varying opinions on healthcare systems, such as the move towards universal versus private healthcare models, often align with generational experiences and expectations.

7. The Role of Government:

This is a heated debate these days.

Opinions on the appropriateness of government intervention and regulation in individuals' lives can significantly differ across age groups.

However, this divide is coming closer as some of the other topics mentioned have brought each group into conflict with governments over their respective issues. Even though the groups and issues differ, the governments they conflict with are the same.

8. *Military and Foreign Policy:*

Perspectives on military engagement and foreign policy may be influenced by the generational impact of events like the Vietnam War, the Cold War, 9/11, and the wars in Afghanistan and Iraq.

More recently, the situations in Ukraine and Gaza have caused generational divisions regarding stances.

9. *Race Relations:*

Generational differences in attitudes towards race can be significant, shaped by the Civil Rights movements of the past and current discussions on systemic racism and now the Black Lives Matter movement.

10. *Economic Policies:*

Opinions on taxation, welfare, and government spending can be heavily influenced by the economic climate of each generation's formative years.

11. Climate Change and Environmental Policy:

Younger generations are typically more engaged with environmental activism, reflecting a growing concern for sustainable living and the impact of climate change on their future.

These topics are influenced by the unique socio-economic and political contexts that define each generation's coming-of-age period, leading to distinct perspectives and priorities. Understanding these generational differences requires open communication and a willingness to see the world through the lens of another age group.

This is challenging, but creating spaces where these topics can be discussed without judgment is essential for promoting understanding across generations. Again, this is another area where open and honest communication is necessary. They can also benefit from all four DSD pillars of *self-awareness*, *resilience*, *authenticity*, and *empathy*. These can help guide us towards being open to understanding one another.

Substance Abuse: The Silent Demon

Issues of addiction and substance abuse for family members can cast a dark shadow over the entire family. Trust is shattered, financial strain ensues, and emotional distress permeates every interaction. Confronting the uncomfortable truth of addiction is a painful but necessary step toward healing and rebuilding the family's foundation.

Financial Problems: The Weight of Money

Money issues, whether stemming from debt, differing spending habits, or disputes over inheritances, can create significant stress and conflict within families. Financial stability is often intertwined with emotional well-being, and when these issues go unaddressed, they can erode the family's sense of security and unity. Open and honest conversations about finances are essential for finding common ground and ensuring the family's financial health.

Mental Health Issues: The Unseen Struggle

Mental health struggles of one or more family members, especially if not openly discussed or adequately addressed, can strain family relationships and dynamics. The stigma surrounding mental health often prevents individuals from seeking help, leading to a cycle of suffering and isolation. Creating a safe space for open dialogue and providing support is crucial for fostering understanding and promoting healing.

Infidelity and Marital Strife: The Cracks in the Foundation

Infidelity or ongoing marital conflicts can fracture the very foundation of the family unit. The betrayal and emotional turmoil accompanying these issues create a tense and unstable environment, affecting every family member. Addressing the uncomfortable truths at the heart of these conflicts is necessary to rebuild trust and restore family harmony.

Infidelity is tough; if not dealt with, it leads to the next.

Divorce and Separation: The Breaking Point

Sometimes, it's the only way and for the best. However, divorce or separation and the subsequent restructuring of family life can unearth uncomfortable truths and create conflicts. Unraveling a once-united unit can expose hidden resentments and unresolved issues, forcing family members to confront painful truths about themselves and their relationships. Navigating this tumultuous terrain requires open communication, *empathy*, and a commitment to finding a new equilibrium.

Favoritism and Sibling Rivalry: The Battle for Love

Parents' perceived favoritism can sow the seeds of long-standing sibling rivalries, leaving scars that persist into adulthood. The emotional toll of feeling inadequate and unloved can create a toxic dynamic within the family, breeding resentment and discord. Acknowledging and addressing these uncomfortable truths is essential for healing the wounds of the past and fostering a sense of equality and love among siblings.

Cultural and Identity Conflicts: The Clash of Worlds

In multicultural families or cases where family members have different views on cultural identity, conflicts can arise regarding traditions, customs, and lifestyles. The clash of worlds can create a divide within the family as individuals struggle to reconcile their own identities with the expectations and traditions of their heritage. Embracing diversity, fostering open dialogue, and finding common ground are vital for bridging these cultural gaps.

Secrets and Lies: The Hidden Truths

Family secrets, whether they involve hidden relationships, undisclosed financial matters, or health issues, can erode trust and create a breeding ground for resentment. The weight of these hidden truths can strain relationships and hinder genuine connection. Uncovering and addressing these uncomfortable truths is essential for rebuilding trust and fostering authentic relationships within the family.

Expectations and Pressures: The Weight of Perfection

Unrealistic or unmet expectations regarding career, education, or personal choices can cause strain between family members. The pressure to live up to perceived standards can create a suffocating environment, stifling individuality and breeding resentment. Embracing open communication and setting realistic expectations is crucial for fostering understanding and supporting each other's unique paths.

Caregiving for Aging Parents: The Burden of Time

I wanted to revisit this as the last thing we discuss in this chapter because I want it to stay with you and your mindset. Again, please know that I understand all families, all parents, and all relationships with our parents are different. However, as adults now who have our own families or simply from life experiences, see if you can let go of past trauma and drama and have the final memories with your parents be memorable ones.

I know that the responsibilities and challenges of caring for elderly family members can strain relationships and create conflicts, especially if the burden is unevenly distributed among family members.

It's hard, I know. But try.

In summary, recognizing and addressing these uncomfortable truths within families is a significant step towards healing and strengthening the bonds that tie you together. It's worth it.

Chapter End Notes

Chapter 11:

DSD.
into Health and Wellness.

BE AUTHENTIC WITH YOURSELF.

Stay energized.
Never stop stop moving forward.

@DEEPSHALLOWDIVE

Chapter 11: DSD into Health and Wellness.

Let's bring it home on a solid note. This is the final chapter before we get to the *Summary* and *Conclusions*. I also wanted to end with this topic because it is another one near and dear to me and another area where I would love to provide some value to you: Health and Wellness.

They also say that people remember the ending of books the most.

Even though I hope you remember all areas of this book, if I can make you more mindful and aware of your health and help you stay healthy, you can always return to all these other areas.

Always remember the adage, 'The greatest wealth is health.' From the simple wisdom of 'an apple a day keeps the doctor away' to the profound realization that your body is a temple that must be worshipped daily- these ideas reinforce the invaluable asset of good health.

I have created a series of podcast episodes under the *DSD Health* moniker, so you will see another QR code at the end of this chapter.

Since an entire book could be dedicated to health and wellness, you can listen to those episodes and continue learning through the podcast.

Embarking on a track toward health and wellness can often feel overwhelming. With so much conflicting information and fleeting fads, it's not easy to lose weight, but it is easy to lose sight of the core principles underpinning a healthy lifestyle.

In this chapter, we will again apply the DSD methodology to uncover the essence of health and wellness through *self-awareness*, *resilience*, *authenticity*, and *empathy*.

Self-Awareness: Your Health, Your Narrative

Remember, *self-awareness* is the initial cornerstone pillar of DSD. Like in a relationship, developing a *deep*, reflective understanding of your health is crucial. Listening to your body's cues after a meal, during exercise, or post-sleep reveals insights essential for health optimization.

Monitoring your health markers—such as weight, blood pressure, and blood work—is a practice in *self-awareness*. It's about understanding your baseline to make informed, health-enhancing decisions.

Resilience: Building Your Health House

Resilience in health means adopting habits and routines that stand the test of time and challenges. It's about establishing a regimen that accommodates setbacks and adapts to change. Whether incorporating a new dietary habit or a workout routine, *resilience* is about the commitment to persist and adapt, embodying the philosophy that fitness is not a destination; it's a way of life.

Even though it is cliché when people say it's not a diet, it's a lifestyle, it's true. Once that switch flicks for you and your health becomes top of mind, you will have the *resilience* to keep improving.

The problem is that people often need a health scare or an incident to wake them up to this, but hopefully, this book and the podcast episodes on health can play that role for you so that you are proactive and not reactive.

Authenticity: Aligning Actions with Values

Authenticity in your health journey involves aligning your actions with your core values and authentic self. It's choosing a diet or exercise not because it's trendy but because you believe in it.

Embrace activities that you genuinely enjoy and make them the mainstays of your health regimen, ensuring that your path to wellness is tailored to your needs.

The podcast episodes will discuss this and various topics, from Intermittent Fasting to Walking to paying attention to the deposits you make into the toilet when you go to the bathroom.

Remember, at the beginning of this book, I promised to keep it real and raw; well, if nothing else, I am a man of my word! There is an entire episode on the podcast that you can listen to that talks about how to interpret what your #1 and #2 mean. No cap. Google that term if you need to!

Empathy: Understanding and Compassion in Your Health Journey

Empathy, in this case, self-empathy, is pivotal in navigating wellness. It's about treating yourself with kindness and understanding, especially on challenging days.

Empathy allows you to acknowledge your struggles without harsh judgment, fostering a nurturing environment for change and growth.

As we culminate this chapter with a reflection on health and wellness, remember that this is more than just a chapter in a book—it's an invitation to embark on a lifelong path of well-being guided by the principles and pillars of the *Deep Shallow Dive* methodology.

Your awakening journey and path to health are unique.

They are illuminated by a *deep* understanding of self and the adoption of practices that resonate with your innermost needs and values.

Start tracking your health. I talked about several things to track and several ways to track your health before, and I call this *Body Data*.

Keeping track of your daily habits—what you eat, how much you move, and how you rest—helps you notice patterns and listen to your body's responses.

This self-reflection will provide a foundation for understanding your unique health needs and body data.

Next, equip yourself with knowledge about nutrition, exercise, and mindfulness. Understand the science behind these topics, but don't get lost in the details. Focus on fundamental principles and apply them to your choices. This preparation will help guide you toward making informed choices.

It's essential to approach changes in your health habits with positivity and curiosity rather than as a punishment for past habits. Set an inviting tone for yourself as you commit to one change at a time.

Whether integrating more protein into your diet or adding a daily walk to your routine, start small but stay consistent. Be actively engaged in your health-related actions. When eating, savor the flavors of each bite; when exercising, feel the movement of your body; and when resting, embrace stillness fully.

Find activities you genuinely enjoy and incorporate them into your wellness routine. Health doesn't have to feel like a chore. If you love dancing, make it part of your exercise regimen. But as I tell everyone, start with one thing we all can hopefully do: walk.

Walking is the most important thing you can do consistently and daily.

Again, at the end of this chapter, I will share a QR code for the dedicated DSD Health episodes, with Walking being EP#93, which you can listen to as part of your diving-in process.

Establish goals that resonate with you.

What does health mean to you?

Is it the ability to run a 5K or the mental clarity needed to be productive?

Define what health looks like for you and create a roadmap of small, achievable steps that lead towards your larger goal.

Again, seek forward momentum.

When setbacks occur, use humor to lighten the situation. Allow setbacks to be learning opportunities rather than reasons to give up. Respect your boundaries and know your limits.

Pushing yourself too hard can lead to burnout or injury, hindering your progress toward better health.

Be patient with yourself throughout this process. Lasting change takes time. Remember that each step forward, no matter how small, is a step towards a healthier and more fulfilling life.

Forward momentum.

In summary, the true essence of *Deep Shallow Dive* in health and wellness lies in the intersection of depth and simplicity. Apply what you've learned about your body and preferences to create a tailored health plan that includes walking, meal prepping, or training for a fitness goal. Commit to these and commit to yourself.

Since the list of podcast episodes on *Health and Wellness* will continue to grow as we tackle more topics, you can find all these organized in a Series on our website and listen directly there.

Or note the episode number and feel free to find it on Spotify, Apple Podcasts, iHeart, Pandora, Amazon Music, YouTube, and anywhere else you listen to your podcasts:

Chapter End Notes

Chapter 12:

BE AUTHENTIC WITH YOURSELF.

Deep Shallow Dive Into YOU.
Summary and Conclusions.

Stay visionary.
Never stop dreaming big. YOU got this!

@DEEPSHALLOWDIVE

Chapter 12: DSD Into YOU.
Summary and Conclusions.

It's time to wrap everything up, review what we have learned, and make a plan to move forward. In this concluding chapter of *Deep Shallow Dive into YOU*, I want to start by saying thank you.

Thank you for your time.

You took time from your life to read this book instead of all the other things you could have done.

I appreciate that.

I hope that this book has prompted you just to think.

Throughout the book, we have explored various themes and insights that highlight the significance of confronting complex realities to provide growth at an individual and societal level.

We drove home the importance of embracing uncomfortable truths, *calling a Spade a Spade*, and how they can help you have a more authentic relationship with yourself. And I hope you had a few laughs.

I encourage you to reflect on the four pillars of the DSD Methodology as you reflect on this journey and always keep those in mind.

Remember, it all starts with *Self-awareness* and acknowledgment. Recognizing uncomfortable truths within ourselves and the world around us is crucial, such as discrimination, inequality, and injustice. This process of acknowledgment catalyzes personal growth and self-improvement. It encourages self-reflection, introspection, and a willingness to challenge our biases and preconceptions.

Throughout the book, we highlighted the importance of *Resilience* and persistence in the face of adversity. Embracing uncomfortable truths can be emotionally challenging, but staying committed to positive change is essential. Building *resilience*, seeking support, and practicing self-care are crucial in sustaining our efforts.

Authenticity and aligning our values with our actions is a transformative process that often begins with acknowledging uncomfortable truths. We can inspire and empower those around us by embracing our true selves and sharing our capabilities and challenges with others.

Lastly, embracing uncomfortable truths also requires *Empathy* and compassion. Understanding the experiences and perspectives of others is vital to fostering *empathy* and building bridges of understanding. It is through *empathy* that we can address uncomfortable truths and drive real change. By understanding others better, we can work toward a more authentic version of ourselves.

To recap, confronting uncomfortable truths is hard but leads to healing and reconciliation within families and personal relationships. Open and honest communication is essential in mending broken bonds and promoting understanding.

Embracing uncomfortable truths brings together individuals who share similar concerns and passions. This sense of community can lead to networks of advocates and activists working towards common goals. By collaborating with others, we can amplify our impact and advocate for change on a larger scale.

Embracing uncomfortable truths contributes to cultural shifts in attitudes and beliefs. It challenges stereotypes, biases, and norms that perpetuate discrimination and inequality. We can act as catalysts for cultural change by questioning societal norms and practices. By staying informed about international issues and engaging in geopolitical conversations, we can contribute to positive change worldwide.

Embracing uncomfortable truths is a transformative process that requires self-reflection, accountability, and a commitment to positive change. Through *self-awareness*, *resilience*, *empathy*, and *authenticity*, you can implement the DSD Methodology and the concepts of embracing uncomfortable truths in your own lives. Please continue your personal growth by applying this book's key themes and insights.

Remember, in your evolution, there will come times when you must confront things about yourself. These truths may challenge your beliefs, expose your vulnerabilities, and force you to reevaluate your choices. Yet, it is through embracing these uncomfortable truths that you can experience true transformation.

Whether you are dealing with Politics, Personal Relationships, Social Issues, Family Life, or Health and wellness, I hope you have learned valuable practices from this book.

Lastly, I want to leave you with the *DSD Methodology Reflection Guide* as a parting gift. This is a series of questions designed to help you delve even deeper into the book's critical themes by applying the principles of DSD while anchoring your mindset in the pillars of *Self-awareness, Resilience, Authenticity,* and *Empathy*.

As you embark on your journey of self-discovery and personal growth, I encourage you to utilize the *Room Reflection Pages* provided at the end of this book. In those pages, you'll find space to capture your answers and thoughts to the *DSD Methodology Reflection Guide* questions and any additional insights or reflections you wish to document from your reading experience. Take opportunities to dive deeper into your inner landscape, charting your thoughts and discoveries. Embrace the discomfort, celebrate the moments of clarity, and trust in the transformative power of self-reflection.

Your journey starts here:

DSD Methodology Reflection Guide

Self-awareness:

1.　What uncomfortable truths about yourself have you been avoiding?

2.　Are there surface-level behaviors or habits that mask deeper issues?

3.　What steps can you take to delve deeper into your motivations, fears, and desires?

Resilience:

1.　When faced with adversity or discomfort, how do you typically respond?

2.　Do you find yourself avoiding discomfort or seeking quick fixes to avoid facing challenges?

3.　How can you summon the strength to persevere when faced with significant setbacks or obstacles?

Authenticity:

1.　Are there aspects of yourself that you've been hiding or suppressing?

2.   Are there areas of your life where you conform to societal expectations rather than being true to yourself?

3.   In what areas of your life do you feel the most pressure to conform to societal norms or expectations?

Empathy:

1.   How well do you understand the perspectives and experiences of others?

2.   Are you actively listening to others' viewpoints, or are you quick to dismiss or invalidate them?

3.   Can you *call a Spade a Spade* on yourself when you are being close-minded and not giving others a chance?

These questions prompt thoughtful reflection and facilitate a deeper understanding of yourself.

In conclusion, as we deepen our understanding of uncomfortable truths, we become agents of change, committed to personal growth and internal transformation.

Through these uncomfortable truths, we can truly understand ourselves and the world.

So, let us embark on this journey of self-discovery.

Let us embrace the truth with everything.

Let us embrace the reality of the world.

Let us embrace change in our lives.

Remember that having integrity is crucial in our lives, even if it can sometimes be challenging and demanding. However, it can serve as our guiding light and keep us on track to living a life of love and honor.

Finally, let's never forget to *Call a Spade a Spade!*

Thank you again for allowing me the chance to guide you through this *Deep Shallow Dive into YOU.*

The End.

In a World where YOU can be anything...

be Kind

Chapter End Notes

About the Author

RAY DOUSTDAR
ENTREPRENEUR. PODCAST HOST. AUTHOR.

Ray Doustdar is a dynamic entrepreneur and innovative thinker who has made significant waves in the health and wellness industry, as well as in the podcasting world. As the CEO and Founder of **BUICED Liquid Vitamins**, Ray has revolutionized the way people think about and consume vitamins, offering a unique liquid solution that prioritizes bioavailability and convenience. His passion for health and dedication to providing a superior product have positioned **BUICED** as a leader in the dietary supplement market.

Beyond his success in the health sector, Ray has also made a name for himself in the realm of digital media. As the founder of the **Deep Shallow Dive Podcast**, he has created a platform that delves into the minds of various thought leaders, innovators, and influencers, offering listeners a unique blend of deep insights and lighthearted conversation. His natural charisma and inquisitive nature make him an engaging host, and the podcast has quickly become a favorite among those who appreciate thoughtful discourse, genuine storytelling, and calling a spade a spade, which has become synonymous with the **DSD**.

Adding a new chapter to his diverse career, Ray is now a debut author with the release of **'Deep Shallow Dive into You.'** This book fosters personal growth and self-awareness. It offers readers a transformative journey to cultivate a more authentic relationship with themselves. Ray aims to connect with readers profoundly through his writing, sharing insights and strategies to help them live with unwavering authenticity and intention.

> **Sometimes later becomes never.
> Do it now.**

...and he always tries to **Call a Spade a Spade!**

Acknowledgments.

This book has been informed and enriched by countless articles and reports from numerous esteemed news organizations worldwide. I extend my gratitude to the following outlets, among others, for their dedication to journalism and for providing the public with reliable and comprehensive news coverage that has significantly contributed to the research and knowledge behind this work.

United States: The New York Times, The Washington Post, The Wall Street Journal, CNN, NBC News, CBS News, ABC News, Fox News, NPR (National Public Radio), USA Today, Bloomberg, Politico, The Atlantic, The New Yorker, TIME, The Intercept, AP News, Axios, the Epoch Times.

United Kingdom: BBC (British Broadcasting Corporation), The Guardian, The Times, The Telegraph, Financial Times, Sky News.

Canada: CBC (Canadian Broadcasting Corporation), The Globe and Mail, National Post, CTV News.

Australia: ABC (Australian Broadcasting Corporation), The Sydney Morning Herald, The Australian, SBS (Special Broadcasting Service).

Europe: Der Spiegel (Germany), Le Monde (France), El País (Spain), The Economist (UK, International), RTE (Ireland).

Asia: NHK (Japan), The Times of India, South China Morning Post (Hong Kong), Al Jazeera (Qatar, International), Hindustan Times (India).

Latin America: Folha de S.Paulo (Brazil), Clarín (Argentina).

Africa: Daily Nation (Kenya), The Mail & Guardian (South Africa).

International: Reuters, Associated Press, Agence France-Presse, Bloomberg, Financial Times (UK, International), CNN International, Al Jazeera English.

This book also benefited from many top websites consistently providing comprehensive and reliable daily news. These outlets have been instrumental in offering up-to-date information that has helped shape the content of this work.

CNN, BBC News, The New York Times, The Guardian, The Washington Post, Reuters, Al Jazeera, Fox News, NBC News, ABC News, CBS News, HuffPost, CNBC, The Wall Street Journal, Bloomberg, Politico, NPR (National Public Radio), USA Today, Los Angeles Times, All Sides Media.

Room for Reflections

Room for Reflections

...remember to call a spade a spade!

Room for Reflections

www.ingramcontent.com/pod-product-compliance
Lightning Source LLC
Chambersburg PA
CBHW060040030426
42334CB00019B/2409